NORTHERN GOSHAWK
THE GRAY GHOST
Habits, Habitat, and Rehabilitation

Written and Illustrated by Scott Rashid

Other Schiffer Books by the Author:

Small Mountain Owls, ISBN 978-0-7643-3282-1

The Great-Horned Owl: An In-depth Study, ISBN 978-0-7643-4766-5

Published by Schiffer Publishing, Ltd.
4880 Lower Valley Road
Atglen, PA 19310
Phone: (610) 593-1777; Fax: (610) 593-2002
E-mail: Info@schifferbooks.com

For our complete selection of fine books on this and related subjects, please visit our website at www.schifferbooks.com. You may also write for a free catalog.

This book may be purchased from the publisher. Please try your bookstore first.

We are always looking for people to write books on new and related subjects. If you have an idea for a book, please contact us at proposals@schifferbooks.com.

Schiffer Publishing's titles are available at special discounts for bulk purchases for sales promotions or premiums. Special editions, including personalized covers, corporate imprints, and excerpts can be created in large quantities for special needs. For more information, contact the publisher.

Copyright © 2016 by Scott Rashid

Library of Congress Control Number: 2015950980

All rights reserved. No part of this work may be reproduced or used in any form or by any means—graphic, electronic, or mechanical, including photocopying or information storage and retrieval systems—without written permission from the publisher.

The scanning, uploading, and distribution of this book or any part thereof via the Internet or via any other means without the permission of the publisher is illegal and punishable by law. Please purchase only authorized editions and do not participate in or encourage the electronic piracy of copyrighted materials.
"Schiffer," "Schiffer Publishing, Ltd. & Design," and the "Design of pen and inkwell" are registered trademarks of Schiffer Publishing, Ltd.

Designed by RoS
Cover design by Molly Shields
Type set in Caflisch Script Pro/Bell MT

ISBN: 978-0-7643-4990-4
Printed in China

Cover painting by Scott Rashid

For my mother, Joan Rashid,
and in memory of my father, Edward (Jed) Rashid

Scott Rashid's work with Northern Goshawks began after he moved to Colorado in 1998. Since then he has located several Northern Goshawk nests in and around Rocky Mountain National Park. He has spent countless hours with this intrepid hunter, both through research and rehabilitating injured birds. He has worked with numerous bird species from hummingbirds to eagles. Scott's photographs and art are published in two of his other books—*Small Mountain Owls* and *The Great Horned Owl: An In-depth Study*. In 1994, he started a banding station at the YMCA of the Rockies, just south of Estes Park, Colorado, and in 2014, banded his 10,000[th] bird there. He is also director of the Colorado Avian Research and Rehabilitation Institute (CARRI), www.carriep.org.

Contents

Foreword 6
Preface 7
Acknowledgements 7
Introduction 8

Chapter One
My First Encounter 11
Anatomy 13
Distinguishing Among the Three Accipters 15
What's in a Name? 18
Habitat and Territory Size 18
Distribution 20

Chapter Two
Vocalization 21
Courtship 23
Hunting and Food Habits 23
Plucking Posts and Pellets 32

Chapter Three
Nest Characteristics 37
Eggs and Incubation 48
Nesting and Nest Defense 50
Nestlings 76
Fledging and Post-Fledging 82

Chapter Four
Northern Goshawks in Fall and Winter 93
Rehabilitation 98
Mortality and Longevity 103
Predation by Animals and Other Birds 104

Scientific Names of Birds, Plants, and Animals 106
References 110

Foreword

I've been in the field with Scott Rashid numerous times. He's good. He *sees* things. In this book you can go with him, too—to explore the world of Northern Goshawks —and you don't need a hard hat to protect your head from their defensive attacks!

As he did in his previous works, *Small Mountain Owls* and *The Great Horned Owl: An In-depth Study*, Scott displays the best of a recent, gratifying trend in wildlife conservation—the emergence of citizen science as a valuable source of knowledge needed to protect our natural world. A college professor once told me, "When all else fails, overwhelm your question with data," and citizen-scientists such as Scott are doing just that. With hundreds of thousands of hours of observation data, perhaps millions more data points than professional wildlife biologists could ever hope to achieve, citizen-scientists add to our knowledge of the life requirements of hundreds of species. They document how species are faring in the face of changing landscapes and climate and provide insight into their resilience, or lack thereof, to those changes. In producing *The Northern Goshawk, The Gray Ghost*, Scott exhaustively researched the works of others, identified the knowledge gaps, and then headed to the field to fill in those gaps. Now he is sharing his findings, carefully integrated with those of his predecessors, and substantially advancing our understanding and appreciation of this raptor.

Scott takes things a couple of steps further than most with his combination of written observations and unique artwork. In both, his style is evocative of the broad natural history investigations and illustrations of old-time naturalists. Just as one readily recognizes a bird painting by Audubon, or Fuertes, once you've seen a painting or two by Scott, you'll instantly identify his others, they are that unique and instructive. So enjoy the writing, artwork, and photographs; appreciate the author's passion and talent, his "naturalist's heart" so evident throughout; and above all, come to know this finely adapted forest bird-of-prey, the Northern Goshawk. You will learn much.

—Gary C. Miller
Retired, former statewide ecologist and research leader. Colorado Division of Wildlife (now Colorado Parks and Wildlife), former wildlife biologist, Rocky Mountain National Park

Preface

Few North American bird species have evoked more emotion than the largest of the woodland hawks, the Northern Goshawk. It is one of the more controversial birds in the country due to its ability to hunt some of the same species of birds and animals that we humans raise for food and hunt for sport. The hawks are quite large, yet are difficult to observe because they often live and raise their families far from human habitation.

Northern Goshawks are aggressive predators, capturing birds and animals as large and even larger and heavier than themselves. Game birds such as grouse and ducks, along with animals like ground squirrels and rabbits, are favorite prey. During the nesting season, they construct large stick nests and often relentlessly attack anything that ventures too close to their nests and/or young (Sutton, 1925, Gromme, 1935).

Many years ago, the Red-tailed Hawk erroneously gained the nickname Chicken Hawk. This was because a farmer finding the remains of a chicken on his property would assume that the Red-tailed Hawk soaring above was the culprit. Red-tailed Hawks are capable of killing chickens; but when chickens are taken by large raptors during the day, the perpetrator, more often than not, is either the Northern Goshawk or the Cooper's Hawk. In chapter two you will read about Northern Goshawks taking domestic fowl. All raptors love the taste of chicken, duck, pigeon, and quail, yet few species are as well-equipped to take these species as the Northern Goshawk.

Acknowledgments

I would like to thank Eric Adams, Paul Bannick, Heidi Bucknam, Jeff Connor, Alex Cruz, Anne and John Donovan, Lisa and Matt Dragon, Marsha Hobert, Joe Heyen, Wayne and Diana Johnston, Joe Halt, Gary Mathews, Gary C. Miller, Anita Prinzmetal, Gene Putney, Susan Rashid, Richard Reynolds, Bill Schmoker and the National Park Service at Rocky Mountain National Park.

Introduction

In high school, a friend asked me to create a drawing with Wood Ducks as the main subject matter. He wanted to give the drawing to his father for Father's Day. While searching magazines for reference material, I came upon an article about the Northern Goshawk. The article described the species' fearless nature. As a student just becoming familiar with martial arts, this intrigued me. Soon after reading that article, I received a copy of Arthur Bent's *Life Histories of North American Birds of Prey*, Part One. While reading the section about Northern Goshawks, I became enthralled with the species, and for the next several years I read everything I could find about them.

The most fascinating thing about these hawks is their intense aggression when both hunting and defending their young. I've been around nesting Northern Goshawks when the female has attacked me incessantly, while others seemed not to notice my presence. In my opinion, Northern Goshawks are incapable of counting to more than one or two and get very upset when too many people come near their nests simultaneously. When this happens the adults become aggressive.

While moving to and from nesting Northern Goshawks, I've learned to hold my camera tripod a few inches above my head so that attacking hawks are unable to strafe my head. They pass over the tripod instead and neither the hawk nor I get hurt.

Northern Goshawks are relentless when pursuing prey. Away from their nests they are notorious for chasing likely victims near people's homes and even into them as their prey tries to evade capture. In fall and winter they often prey upon creatures they wouldn't normally find near their nests. Some of these include domestic fowl, such as chickens, guinea fowl, and pigeons, and small mammals including house cats (Bent, 1937). In the spring and fall, I've witnessed Northern Goshawks hunting waterfowl near marshes and in cities near parks and zoos.

Northern Goshawks seldom nest close to human habitation and rarely use their nests for more than one year. During nesting season they are rarely seen unless you're researching them. In the East and Midwest, the Northern Goshawks feed heavily upon Ruffed Grouse (Meng, 1959; Sutton, 1931); in the West they feed mostly on small to medium-size animals including rabbits and squirrels. They're also capable of catching and killing large prey such as hares and turkeys that are considerably heavier than the hawks. In and around Rocky Mountain National Park (RMNP), Northern Goshawks prey on medium-size animals such as ground and tree squirrels, rabbits and hares, and birds ranging from the size of Northern Flickers and Hairy Woodpeckers to larger species including Rock Pigeons and American Crows. During the nesting season, Northern Goshawks use a "plucking post" to prepare their prey before delivering it to their nestlings. This post can be an overhanging branch, large boulder, or even a dead tree stump, where the remains of what the birds fed upon can be found.

In the fall and winter, as individual hawks move far from their nesting grounds, they frequently find themselves in unsatisfactory situations. Inexperienced hawks often get so hungry that they attempt to capture prey that is either too large for them to kill, such as peacocks and peahens, or they hunt too close to homes and businesses where they crash into windows or get hit by cars.

When Northern Goshawks and other birds are injured, ideally they end up at a rehabilitation facility. As a rehabilitator, my first injured Northern Goshawk was an adult male with West Nile Virus. That bird was in rough shape and had to be hand-fed every morning and evening. I had to cut the bird's food into very small pieces and feed him slowly, as he had trouble swallowing. Feeding this hawk took an hour every morning and afternoon. That bird was so sick that he was unable to stand for three weeks. After he began to stand and feed himself, he was on the road to a successful recovery. He was in captivity for six months before I was able to release him back into the wild. I know of no better feeling than taking an injured bird into my care, rehabilitating it, and releasing it back to freedom.

The Northern Goshawk
Accipiter gentilis

Chapter One

My First Encounter

According to the checklist of birds of the ABA (American Birding Association) version 7.7, there are seventeen hawk species nesting throughout North America, including the Osprey. Most of the hawks fit in the buteo category. Buteos are hawks with long, broad wings and relatively short tails. Examples of buteos include Red-tailed Hawks, Broad-winged Hawks, and Swainson's Hawks. These raptors most often hunt forest edges and open country, feeding on small to medium-size animals including voles, rabbits, and ground squirrels.

Also within the hawk family are three species in the accipiter category. The accipiters include the Northern Goshawk, Cooper's Hawk, and Sharp-shinned Hawk. Accipiters, often considered woodland hawks or forest raptors, have short, rounded wings and long tails. Unlike buteos, accipiters are fast-flying birds that live in the woods, feeding on a variety of birds and animals. The largest and most powerful of these forest hawks, the Northern Goshawk, is capable of capturing birds as small as sparrows and woodpeckers and as large as grouse and pheasants. It also feeds on animals as small as voles and chipmunks and as large as squirrels and hares. According to Terres (1982), accipiters are considered by scientists to be one of the many natural checks on small bird populations.

The Northern Goshawk often nests in old-growth forests far from human habitation. Their nesting areas include boreal forests and temperate forests throughout the Northern Hemisphere (Squires and Reynolds, 1997). Growing up in the farm country of south central Wisconsin gave me little chance to see accipiters. However, Red-tailed Hawks and American Kestrels were common. It wasn't until 1982, when I went to college in Stevens Point in central Wisconsin, that I was living in an area where accipiters could routinely be found. That part of Wisconsin is a transition zone between the hardwood forests in the farm country in the southern part of the state and the conifers farther north. The area around Stevens Point has both hardwoods, like maples and oak, and conifers such as white pine and red pine. Cooper's Hawks and Sharp-shinned Hawks nested there. I occasionally heard from friends that the neighborhood Cooper's Hawk would take doves and jays from their bird feeders. In the fall it was common to see large numbers of Cooper's and Sharp-shinned Hawks migrating through the region.

My first encounter with the Northern Goshawk was in 1986, when I went to Northern Wisconsin with Chis Cold, a fellow student at the University of Wisconsin–Stevens Point. For years he had been studying Northern Goshawks and other raptors. He knew of an active Northern Goshawk nest and was going up to band the young. I jumped at the chance.

We drove three and a half hours north, almost to upper Michigan. The forest that the hawks were nesting in was a mixture of hardwoods and conifers. We drove into the woods along the forest service road as far as we could. Then we walked a mile (1.60 km) or so to get to the nest.

Most of the time, when you get anywhere close to a Northern Goshawk nest, the female will come out and introduce herself by flying at you and cackling, hoping to frighten you away. This particular female did just that. We heard the distinctive cak-cak-cak-cak-

Falcons like the American Kestrel have long, pointed wings and a long tail for fast flight in open country.

Accipiters like the Sharp-shinned Hawk have short, rounded wings and a long tail for maneuvering through dense foliage.

cak well before we were even in view of her nest. After we took a few more steps, we could hear the cackling coming toward us. Within seconds she flew directly at us and passed overhead, landing on a pine behind us. I remember her being a large hawk with a beautiful blue-gray back, pale gray breast and belly, blood-red eyes, and a long tail.

I stood for several minutes admiring her beauty and immense size, as she glared at us. While we were watching her, she was scanning the surrounding area, seemingly looking to see how many of us were in the immediate area. After a few moments, we continued moving in the direction she came from when Chris spotted her nest several feet off the ground against the trunk of a conifer. Unfortunately, her chicks were younger than Chris had expected and too small to band. We took a few minutes to search for any prey remains before we made our way back to the car. It was exhilarating to have seen such a magnificent bird of prey.

Since moving to Northern Colorado in 1989, I have seen countless Northern Goshawks and located several nests. During the nesting season these magnificent raptors can be found in the higher-elevation forests. Yet as birds disperse after the nesting season, they are found virtually anywhere from large cities like Denver and Boulder to grasslands far from their mountain habitat.

Buteos like the Red-tailed Hawk have large, broad wings and a broad tail for soaring in open country.

An adult female Northern Goshawk in Rocky Mountain National Park.

Anatomy

Adult Northern Goshawks are about the size of Common Ravens. Both species are roughly 2 feet (.61 m) from head to tail. Adult female Northern Goshawks, larger than males, measure 21–24 inches (53–62 cm) from head to tail, have a wingspan of 41–45 inches (98–104 cm) and weigh between 26–43 ounces (758–1,214 g). The smaller males are 18–20 inches from head to tail (46–51 cm) and have a wingspan of 38–41 inches (98–104 cm). Males weigh 24–36 ounces (677–1,014 g) (Wheeler and Clark, 1995).

An adult Northern Goshawk is an overall slate blue-gray to brown-gray color, including the top of the head, nape, back, wings, and tail. The under parts, including the under-wings, are barred a light gray. The tail is long, with horizontal dark barring and a white terminal band. Their heads have a dark cap, sometimes appearing black; on some birds they actually are black. There is a pronounced white supercilium (line) above the eyes, and the eyes of the adult birds are orange-red to blood-red. The adults' breast and belly are light gray with fine, gray horizontal barring and black vertical streaks (Squires and Reynolds, 1997). Adult females are often more coarsely barred and browner than males. Under-tail coverts are large, white, and fluffy. Their feet, cere (fleshy portion around the nostrils), legs, and toes are yellow, and their talons are black.

An adult male Northern Goshawk. Males have fine barring on their breasts and bellies.

An adult female Northern Goshawk. Females have coarse barring on their breasts and bellies.

A juvenile Northern Goshawk independent from its parents.

Juvenile birds (no longer dependent on their parents) are an overall brown with white mottling on the back and the upper wing coverts (Wheeler and Clark, 1995). The belly and flanks are heavily streaked with brown, as are the under-tail coverts. These under-tail coverts are less fluffy in juveniles than in adults. Their tails are long with irregular dark bands and light barring above and below each band. Eyes are yellow to orange with a light eye line (supercilium). Their cere, legs, and feet are yellow with black talons.

Distinguishing Among the Three Accipiters

While identifying adult accipiters up close is easy with a bit of study and practice, identifying them in the field can be challenging. As I mentioned earlier, the Northern Goshawk is the largest of the three, about the size of a Common Raven. The Cooper's Hawk is next to largest, about the size of an American Crow, and the smallest, the Sharp-shinned Hawk, is the size of a blue or Steller's Jay. All three species are short-winged, long-tailed, forest-dwelling raptors, with barring on their tails and wings (Wheeler and Clark, 1995).

Differentiating between juvenile Northern Goshawks and juvenile Cooper's Hawks is more difficult than discerning between juvenile Sharp-shinned Hawks and juvenile Northern Goshawks. Cooper's Hawks and Northern Goshawks can appear the same size at times; however, Northern Goshawks are always larger (Wheeler and Clark, 1995). When distinguishing between a perched "coop" (Cooper's Hawk) or "gos" (Northern Goshawk), remember that juvenile Northern Goshawks have the pronounced supercillium, a light-colored line of feathers that extends from the cere (yellow fleshy area around the nostrils) above the eyes. A Northern Goshawk has heavily marked underparts including under-tail coverts. The belly of a Cooper's Hawk, on the other hand, is lightly barred or absent any barring. The tail has short outer feathers, giving the tail a rounded look. Juvenile Cooper's Hawks have a distinctive white terminal band on their tails, whereas Northern Goshawks have a thin white tail band. Also, the under-tails of Cooper's Hawks have even barring, while the under-tails of Northern Goshawks have uneven barring.

With all accipiters, the females are larger than the males, a term called reverse sexual dimorphism. This size difference is most evident in Sharp-shinned Hawks and less so with the Northern Goshawk. Storer (1966) and Reynolds (1972) have discussed the theory of reverse sexual dimorphism and give some plausible reasons for this. In the spring, prior to egg laying, the female Northern Goshawk has to produce enough energy to create a clutch of eggs. Less caloric intake means a smaller clutch size. The female can gain her calories in one of three ways: spend more time hunting, which takes energy, or rely on the male to find food for her, or both. With the ability to both forage for herself and accept food from the male, she is able to generate the energy needed to lay a full clutch of eggs, as well as a second clutch of eggs if the first is destroyed during incubation (Reynolds, 1972).

It has been long understood that the male is the major provider for the family from the onset of incubation through the middle of the nesting stage (Brown and Amadon, 1968; Cade, 1960; Schell, 1958). In this way, the female can concentrate her energy on fledging the greatest number of young. The family's fitness depends on the amount of food that the male delivers to the female during incubation and the amount of food he brings his family after the eggs have hatched. A proficient hunting male would increase the odds of the pair's fledging young successfully. This may be one reason why immature male Northern Goshawks are seldom, if ever, found nesting with either mature or immature females, while immature females have been found nesting with mature males (Reynolds, 1972; Meng, 1951).

The male accipiter's parental instinct is weaker than that of the female (Amadon, 1959). Therefore, the larger female may have evolved to protect the nestlings from possible predation by the male. This threat would be greatest when the young are small. Therefore, the larger and more aggressive female stays with the young to prevent cannibalism. This also allows the female to forage less often and capture larger prey when she does hunt (Reynolds, 1972).

According to Storer (1966), the smallest accipiter, the Sharp-shinned Hawk, has at its disposal a larger number of prey species in its size range, while the Northern Goshawk is able to capture a greater size range of prey. As for the species' enemies, the smaller Sharp-shinned Hawk will fall prey to more species than the Northern Goshawk whose power of attack is greater.

Storer also suggests that during nesting season, the Sharp-shinned Hawk can prey on the largest number of species for optimum caloric intake. Conversely, the female Sharp-shinned Hawk has the largest number of potential predators that can prey upon her or destroy the contents of the nest. The male Sharp-shinned Hawk, who spends little time on the nest, is subsequently less apt to be killed there.

As he is hunting away from the nest, his increased maneuverability, due to his smaller size, may actually balance the disadvantage of the number of potential predators. The reverse sexual dimorphism of the species on its wintering grounds might be useful for both individuals and pairs that are often in areas where their prey is concentrated. Furthermore, having birds of two different sizes would enable the individuals to hunt the same area without competing against each other for food (Storer 1955, 1966, Zink 1989, Bildstein 1992).

A juvenile Sharp-shinned Hawk is identified by its small size (roughly the size of a Blue Jay), flat tail tip, and horizontal barring on the flanks.

A juvenile Cooper's Hawk is identified by its large size (roughly the size of an American Crow), rounded tail tip, and tear-drop barring on belly and flanks.

A juvenile Northern Goshawk is identified by its large size (roughly the size of a Common Raven), pale eye stripe, and fluffy white under-tail.

Three juvenile accipiters in flight.

What's in a Name?

Whenever you see a bird or animal's name beginning with greater, lesser, northern, southern, and so on, there is at least one other creature with a similar name. For example, there are Greater Yellow-legs and Lesser Yellow-legs, Eastern Wood-Pewee and Western Wood-Pewee. Similarly, there are more than twenty-five species in the goshawk clan worldwide. Some of these include the Crested Goshawk, African Goshawk, Black Goshawk, Gray Goshawk, Brown Goshawk, Eastern Chanting Goshawk, and Frances' Goshawk, to name just a few.

All hawks are in the family *Accipitridae*. Accipere or accipiter originates from the Latin meaning to seize or grasp. The more common word, hawk, comes from the Middle English hauk and the Anglo-Saxon word hafac meaning "having" (Wells 2002).

During the Middle Ages, before the invention of guns, falconry or hawking was a sport in which every class of society participated. Your status determined the species of hawk, eagle, or falcon that you could possess. For example, an emperor would fly a Golden Eagle, but a king would fly a Gyrfalcon, and so on down to servants and children who would fly kestrels.

Goshawks were flown by gentlemen or noblemen, which is where the bird's scientific name, *Accipiter gentilis*, comes from, *gentilis* meaning gentry or noble. Together, the bird's scientific name literally means a bird of prey of nobility (The Peregrine Fund). The common name, goshawk, is derived from Goose Hawk because the medieval falconers routinely used them to hunt geese.

Throughout North America there are three recognized subspecies of Northern Goshawk: Northern Goshawk (*A.g. atricapillus*), Queen Charlotte Goshawk (*A.g. laingi*), and Apache Goshawk (*A.g. apache*) (USDI Fish and Wildlife Service, 1997). Over the years, the Northern Goshawk has earned several nicknames, including Grouse Hawk, Partridge Hawk, Gray Hawk, Cook's Hawk, and Goose Hawk.

Habitat and Territory Size

The North American Northern Goshawk's preferred habitat comprises three areas: the nest area, post-fledging area, and foraging area (Reynolds et al., 1992). Throughout their range, they can be found nesting in a variety of forest types (Reynolds et al., 1992; Graham et al., 1999). Around Rocky Mountain National Park (RMNP) in Colorado, Northern Goshawks are found breeding in the higher mountains above 8,000 feet (2,439 m) within old-growth forests composed of various combinations of ponderosa pine, quaking aspen, lodgepole pine, subalpine spruce, Engleman spruce, and Douglas fir, often with an active water source nearby.

Shuster (1980) studied Northern Goshawk nests in the Arapaho and Roosevelt National Forests and Rocky Mountain National Park between 1971 and 1977. He found that the lowest elevation for a nest was almost 7,400 feet (2,255 m), while the highest was over 9,800 feet (2,664 m). The habitat was a mixture of ponderosa pine, quaking aspen, lodgepole pine, antelope bitterbrush, and sage.

In Utah, Northern Goshawks live in habitat types ranging from pinyon/juniper forests adjacent to grass and shrublands to sub-alpine environments consisting primarily of Engleman spruce and sub-alpine fir forests. Along with the aforementioned tree types, quaking aspen is an important cover for Northern Goshawks. This type of forest ranges from 4,000–11,000 feet (1,219 m–3,354 m) (Graham, et al.,1999).

In the eastern United States, Northern Goshawks prefer nesting in mature mixed deciduous forests comprised of birch, beech, maple, and hemlock (Speiser and Bosakowski, 1987). In Wisconsin, Rosenfield et al. (1998) found Northern Goshawks in a variety of forest stands including pine plantations, upland maple and maple-oak woodlands, black ash swamps, and aspens.

Typical Northern Goshawk habitat in Rocky Mountain National Park.

Northern Goshawks prefer old-growth forests with large trees, downed logs, and an open understory.

In the western United States, Northern Goshawks are often found in mixed ponderosa pine and spruce-fir forests. The Northern Goshawk's nesting home range is roughly 6,000 acres (Reynolds et al.,1992).

Distribution

In the Americas, Northern Goshawks breed from northwestern Alaska to the northwestern portions of Mackenzie in northern Ontario, north central Quebec, northern Labrador and Newfoundland, and south along the Pacific Coast including the western islands of Kodiak, Queen Charlotte, and Vancouver. They also inhabit the mountains of northern and western Washington, western Oregon including the Cascades and Siskiyou Mountains, and south through central California. They are in western and southern Montana, along with parts of Idaho, south through Wyoming, Utah, and in the mountains of Nevada and western Colorado. Moreover, they are found throughout north central New Mexico and northeastern and southwestern Arizona. The species is found nesting in the Black Hills of South Dakota and from the Canadian Border south into central Minnesota, Wisconsin, and throughout upper Michigan and the northern section of the lower peninsula of Michigan, parts of Pennsylvania, northwestern New Jersey, southeastern New York, western and northern Connecticut, and southeastern Massachusetts. The Northern Goshawk also breeds in parts of the Appalachians and east West Virginia.

The species' winter range extends through most of the western states into North and South Dakota through southern Minnesota, northern Illinois, northern Indiana east through northwestern Virginia, and east to the coast. However, the birds have been documented in all US states in winter, except Hawaii (Sibley, 2000).

The birds also breed in portions of Mexico, according to Howell and Webb (1995): in eastern-most Sonora, the western Chihuahuas, and south to Jalisco.

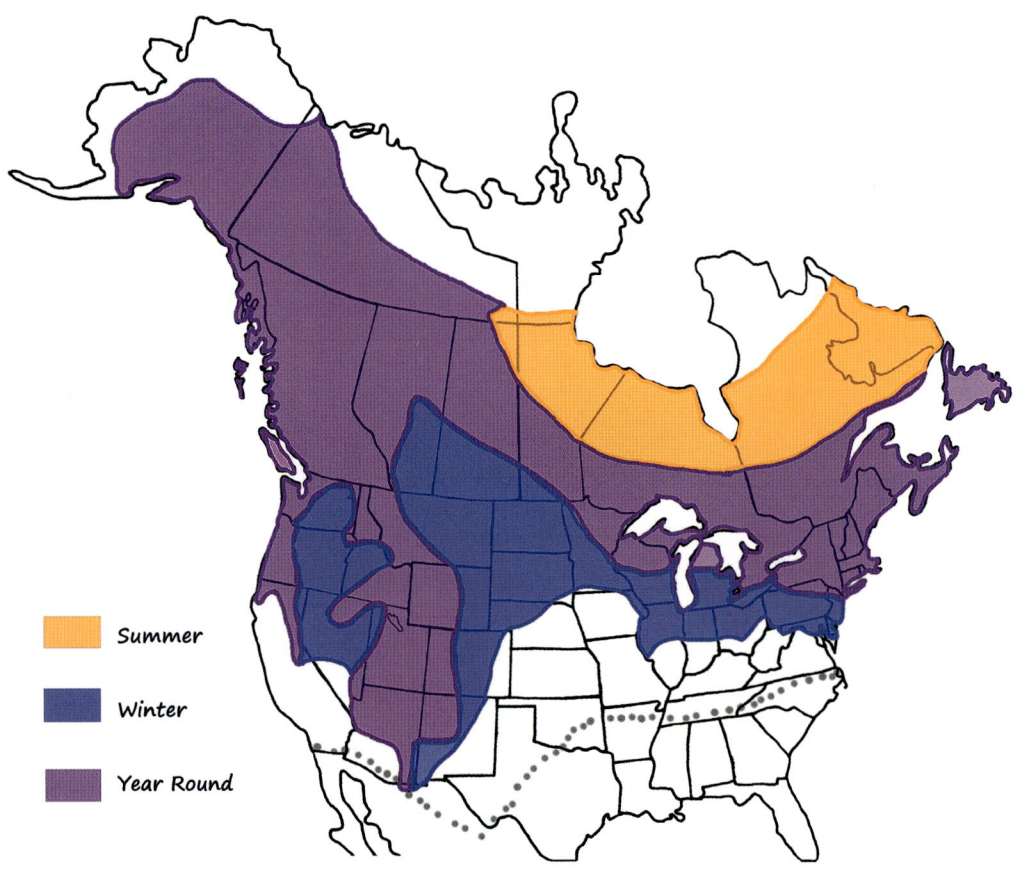

Chapter Two

Vocalization

The only time most people hear the call of a Northern Goshawk is just before one flies near, or even hits them, as they unknowingly approach an active nest. The birds emit a harsh, high-pitched *cac-cac-cac-cac-cac-cac* or *cuk-cuk-cuk-cuk-cuk-cuk*, or even *kek-kek-kek-kek-kek-kek* (Bent, 1937). On occasion, the male will introduce himself as well; his call is similar but lower in pitch.

Most Northern Goshawk vocalization occurs from late winter through early spring, often corresponding with courtship, establishing of their territory, and breeding (Penteriani, 2001). Starting in January, Northern Goshawks become more territorial, often vocalizing when people come close to their nest. They also intensify their vocalization as the young begin to disperse from the nesting area (Penteriani, 2001) in September and early October.

Adult female Northern Goshawk vocalizing as I approached her nest.

The same female, looking at me.

In Bent (1937), a Mr. Tufts wrote: "The usual cry is a strident staccato *cac-cac-cac*, which has a piercing, menacing tone and is uttered rather deliberately. This is the rather common alarm call note as an intruder approaches a nest, and I have never heard it except in the nesting season. In fact, I have never heard a goshawk make any note except at that time."

As the female intensifies her attack, her *kakking* becomes more rapid, almost to the quality of screaming. When the female tires from extended calling, her calls become spaced with longer intervals (Squires, 1997). Gromme (1935) described the battle cry or alarm as "an upscale slurring of two notes resembling the word "gyp" with the accent on the last

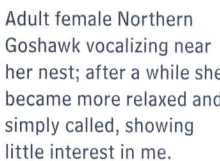

Adult female Northern Goshawk vocalizing near her nest; after a while she became more relaxed and simply called, showing little interest in me.

An adult female Northern Goshawk attacking.

syllable and repeated in rapid succession." When the female wants her mate to bring food for the nestlings, she utters a clear, short, down-scale slurred note, as from "do" to "la" and it has an impatient appealing quality to it. This call sounds similar to that of a Blue Jay."

Both males and females call to each other, uttering a "wail" call (*kree-ah*) that lasts a second or two. This call is given when the male comes near the woods where the nest is located, when the male comes to the nest with food, and when the female leaves the nest after the male has delivered food (Squires,1997).

Sutton (1925) describes a similar call given by the female when the male came to a nest with a black squirrel. "The new note sounds like *Kee-a-ah* and reminded me of the call of the Red-shouldered Hawk, but was more powerful and at the same time more musical, and had a plaintive character that rather affected my sympathy. I sensed immediately that this call indicated a change of some kind in the bird's attitude. Suddenly the dark swiftly flying male appeared bearing in his claws a black squirrel."

Penteriani (2001) found that the commonly heard alarm call or *kek-kek-kek-kek-kek* was also uttered preceding and/or following pair contact, food, and greeting calls. He believed that this call has a twofold meaning, both as alarm and elevated excitement during male contact. He describes the bird's contact call being a *kek . . . kek . . . kek . . .* which was often uttered from the time of establishing territory until the eggs were laid. Therefore he believes that the frequently heard *kek-kek-kek-kek-kek* call is related to anger, stress, or defense of the nest and/or young.

Penteriani (2011) describes the female food-begging call as a *whee-oo . . . whee-oo . . . whee-oo . . .* The females utter this call during incubation and nesting as soon as they hear or see the male around the nest. It may be a kind of recognition call. She also utters this call when the male delivers food, and as a signal to dismiss the male from the area.

Courtship

In some parts of the country individual Northern Goshawks stay on their territory year-round (Squires and Reynolds, 1997). Others, however, make rather long-distance moves in winter, 40.30 miles (65 km) or more from their nests (Squires and Ruggiero, 1995).

Spring migration is apparently poorly understood. However, those birds that have moved from their nesting territory in the fall and winter begin returning in late February (Squires and Reynolds, 1997) through April (Squires and Ruggiero, 1995).

According to Squires and Reynolds (1997), when mated birds return to their territory, they engage in a sky dance that consists of brief soaring flights and the male diving at the female with closed wings above the forest canopy, or a direct aerial chase through the trees. The pair then flies slowly about a meter (3.28 feet) apart with deep, slow wing beats, wings held above body, such as when a Rock Pigeon soars. These initial flights can be shallow or consist of spectacular dives. The pair can be silent during this display or utter wails and chatters. The white under-tail coverts can be flared on either side of the tail as well.

During courtship, copulation occurs with an amazing frequency with over 500 copulations per clutch (Palmer, 1988). According to Moller (1987), copulation peaks early in the nesting cycle, immediately before and during egg laying. Furthermore, copulations occur most frequently in early morning around the time of egg laying and to a lesser extent in the afternoon. The pair will often copulate after the male returns with prey.

Penteriani (2001) found that during courtship, Northern Goshawks would begin vocalizing from one hour before sunrise through the following three hours, with their first calls always being uttered prior to sunrise.

Hunting and Food Habits

One of the more impressive aspects of the bird world is watching a raptor capture its prey. More often than not, it is completely unannounced and depends simply on being in the right place at the right time. Forbush (1927) in Bent (1937) writes: "It's [the goshawks] attack is swift, furious and deadly. In the death grapple it clings ferociously to its victim, careless of its own safety until the unfortunate creature succumbs to its steely grip. Its stroke is terrible. It is delivered with such force as sometimes to tear out most of one side of its victim, and its wing power is so great that it can carry off rabbits and full-grown fowls." Cameron (1907) describes the kill of a Northern Goshawk as "the Goshawk kills its prey by constriction of the feet, and it is quite certain that the squeeze combined with the shock is rapidly fatal to fowls."

When foraging, Northern Goshawks perch in trees and scan the lower canopy of the forest as well as the forest floor for potential prey. A forest with an open understory increases the odds of Northern Goshawks recognizing and capturing prey. This foraging area is approximately 5,400 acres (2,185 ha) (Reynolds et al., 1992).

Several years ago, my wife and I were cutting wood on some private property south of Estes Park, Colorado, above 9,000 feet (2743 m). The forest was comprised of lodgepole, ponderosa, spruce, fir, and aspen. While we were chopping wood, several red squirrels were seemingly announcing their dislike for the noise we were making. A commotion almost 30 feet (9.14 m) up in one of the spruce trees caught my attention. I looked up and saw an adult Northern Goshawk that had just grabbed a red squirrel. I pointed the hawk out to my wife as we watched both hawk and squirrel tumbling through the tree toward the ground. The hawk was able to grasp the squirrel in such a manner that the hawk could fly off before the two of them hit the ground. As the hawk flew off with the hapless squirrel, the other squirrels continued chattering, this time, I suspect, at the hawk, and not us.

Salafsky et al. (2005) found that the Northern Goshawks breeding along the Kaibab Plateau in Arizona fed primarily on red squirrels. They also determined that red squirrels were the only species that had a significant and positive relationship to Northern Goshawk productivity in terms of percent of diet and biomass. Those animals do not hibernate and are diurnal (active during the day), making them the perfect food supply for Northern Goshawks year-round. The Salafsky study determined that, at least along the Kiabab Plateau, Northern Goshawk's productivity was more closely connected with mammalian density than avian density.

On the morning of April 12, 2001, while walking a trail that cuts through a bird sanctuary in Estes Park, Colorado, an adult male Northern Goshawk was walking on the ground in front of me, unaware of my presence as I quietly watched. It reminded me of a bobcat searching the ground for a mouse or other small animal. The hawk looked under several small bushes, almost as if he were sniffing for something. Then he stopped momentarily, and with lightning-fast reflexes, threw his feet forward and grasped a Wyoming ground squirrel by the head and pulled it out of its hole, squeezing it firmly with both feet until the animal was motionless. The hawk looked up, saw me, and flew off carrying the squirrel.

On May 17, 2003, I observed a similar incident while teaching a bird identification class at the YMCA of the Rockies just south of Estes Park. The class consisted of my trapping and banding birds that feed at feeders. Several feeders in this area often have hundreds of birds around them in the spring.

On this afternoon, there were dozens of Red-winged Blackbirds on and around the feeders and in the ponderosas surrounding the feeders. While I was talking to my students, several blackbirds took off from one ponderosa; a few seconds later, another group of blackbirds took off; and then, like they were shot out of a canon, all the birds on the feeders flew off. As the birds flew over our heads, an adult Northern Goshawk caught my eye. It was walking through the sage-covered ground past the feeders, apparently searching for some ground dwelling animal. Unfortunately for the hawk, it flew off without a meal.

W. E. Cram (1899) in Bent (1937) writes of a similar hunting technique. He followed the tracks of a hawk through the woods on the snow; it walked much like a crow, but hopped for a few feet occasionally. At times it followed in the tracks of rabbits for some distance. I have often known them to do this as well and am inclined to think that they occasionally hunt rabbits in this manner where the under-brush is too dense to allow them to fly through it easily. I have sometimes followed their tracks through the brush until I came upon the remains of a freshly killed rabbit.

During the summer of 2004, a pair of Black-billed Magpies had constructed a nest on a limb of a live ponderosa pine between the previously mentioned banding site and the dirt road that leads to one of the housing areas on the YMCA grounds. On July 25 the following year, again while 20 or so students were at the site, adult and juvenile magpies were moving around the area, seemingly talking over the day's activities. Out of the corner of my eye, I noticed a blue-gray "blur" flash in and grasp one of the fledgling magpies and pin it to the ground. This happened within a few yards of the banding site. Immediately, the magpies began a raucous cacophony, scolding the Northern Goshawk with an intensity that you would have to see to believe. Within what seemed like seconds, crows and Steller's Jays joined in on the commotion.

I led the group to better vantage point. The hawk was literally squeezing the life out of the young bird as we watched. Apparently, once the hawk felt the magpie was dead, it flew off carrying its victim, with magpies and crows following behind. Less than a week after that incident, the hawk returned and began chasing the magpies around and through a dense patch of river birch adjacent to the banding site. The magpies squawked violently for several minutes until the hawk flew off. Fortunately for the magpies, the hawk was unsuccessful that time.

Audubon (1840) writes in Bent (1937): "Along the Atlantic coast, this species follows numerous flocks of ducks that are found there during the autumn and winter, and greatly aids in the destruction of Mallards, Teals, Black Ducks and other species, in company with the Peregrine Falcon.

In and around Rocky Mountain National Park, Wyoming, ground squirrels are important food sources for Northern Goshawks.

Adult male Northern Goshawk with a red squirrel.

Red squirrels are a primary food source for Northern Goshawks throughout the Colorado mountains.

"I [Audubon] saw one [Goshawk] abandoning its course to give chase to a large flock of Blackbirds (*Quiscalus versicolor*) [sic], then crossing the river. The hawk approached them with the swiftness of an arrow, when the blackbirds rushed together so closely that the flock looked like a dusky ball passing through the air. On reaching the mass, he, with the greatest ease, seized first one, then another and another, giving each a squeeze with his talons, and suffering it to drop upon the water. In this manner, he had procured four or five before the poor birds reached the woods, into which they instantly plunged, when he gave up the chase, swept over the water in graceful curves, and picked up the fruit of his industry, carrying each bird singly to the shore."

Dr. William Wood of East Windsor Hill, Connecticut, told of a Northern Goshawk that followed a hen into a kitchen and seized her on the kitchen floor in the presence of an old man and his daughter. The father beat the hawk with a cane and finally killed the bold bird. J. A. Farley relates a similar tale from Lambert Lake, Maine. A Goshawk caught a half-grown hen. The escaping hen ran under a woman's skirt. The hawk followed right up to the skirt but was killed. They had to kill the hen, too, for its crop was torn as a result of the hawk's fierce grip (Forbush 1927 in Bent 1937).

Dr. Fisher (1893) in Bent (1937) tells of a farmer who chopped off the head of a fowl and threw the body down beside him. "In an instant a goshawk seized the struggling fowl and flew off with it."

While hunting in Missoula, Montana, Colorado birder Andy Boyce noted a Northern Goshawk taking one of his ducks: "This November (2010) in the Bitteroot Valley in Montana, I was duck hunting along the river and shot a drake Mallard. It hit the ground, twitched its wings three or four times, and got nailed by a Goshawk. Granted, the Goshawk didn't inflict the initial damage, but the intent was certainly there."

Cameron (1907) writes of a Northern Goshawk that grasped and flew off with a Blue-winged Teal as a Mr. Price was hunting ducks. "On October 18, 1905, Mr. Price was after ducks in a snowstorm at his ranch near Knowlton when a Goshawk seizes, and carried past him, a shrieking Blue-winged teal, just as he was on the point of firing at the latter's companion."

During the end of September and early October 1906, Cameron (1907) had four purebred Plymouth Rock Chickens killed by Northern Goshawks. He writes, "The Goshawk, however, invariably flew so low that, like the prowling coyote, it was unperceived until the moment of the fatal dash. Due to the Goshawks hunting near the chicken coop, the chickens learned to stay close to the hen house door. However, on 4 October a Goshawk killed a white hen at the door of the chicken coop. A few days later, a Goshawk killed a rooster. To escape its enemy the terrified fowl had run under some young cedars which would have saved it from a falcon, but were no protection against the relentless Goshawk which followed and seized its prey within the cover."

Over the years, numerous researchers have documented the diet of Northern Goshawks. It is accepted that this species does feed heavily on Ruffed Grouse, in areas where both grouse and hawk are present (Wood, 1938; Latham, 1950; Eng and Guillion, 1962; Squires and Kennedy, Erdman et al., 1998; Smithers et al. 2005). For example, Eng and Gullion (1962) and Fisher (op. cit: 45) comments, "In some parts of the country the Goshawk hunts the Ruffed Grouse so persistently that it is known by the name of 'Partridge Hawk,' and this bird probably has no worse enemy except man." Furthermore, Edminster (1947:197) states, "The goshawk is the one species of predator for which ruffed grouse furnishes a really big proportion of the food."

From the spring of 1956 through the spring of 1961, Eng and Gullion found that of the 232 recorded grouse kills in the Cloquet Forest in Minnesota, Northern Goshawks were the primary predators, with ninety-eight grouse (forty-two percent) being killed. Owls, mostly great horned, took seventeen in the same time frame, with unknown raptors taking nineteen. This data suggests that Northern Goshawks are the single most important

This was the scene at the YMCA of the Rockies as a Northern Goshawk killed a Black-billed Magpie.

factor decimating Ruffed Grouse in that forest. Furthermore, a great number of these Ruffed Grouse taken in the spring were males killed while they were drumming. Identifying whether a Northern Goshawk or Great Horned Owl has taken the grouse, Eng and Gullion determined that white wash (bird feces) and plucked feathers were indications of raptor kills, whereas sheared tail and flight feathers were indications of animal kills. They determined that Northern Goshawks frequently leave the large grouse bones uneaten, such as the sternum and legs, whereas the larger owls seldom leave any scraps of meat or bone.

By looking at recoveries of banded Ruffed Grouse, Eng and Gullion's research (1962) indicated the Northern Goshawks in the Cloquet Forest of Minnesota forage within an area of 3,200 acres or five square miles (13.16 km). They banded grouse at a distance of approximately 3,600 to 8,250 feet (1,098 m to 2,515 m) (average distance of 5,460 feet (1,665 m) from a Northern Goshawk nest. Those grouse were killed by the banded birds, suggesting that Northern Goshawks forage a great distance from their nest.

Besides the grouse, Eng and Gullion (1962) documented Northern Goshawks preying on snowshoe hares, cottontail rabbits, red and flying squirrels, Blue-winged Teal, Common Nighthawk, Pileated Woodpecker, American Robin, Northern Flicker, Blue Jay, Eastern Meadowlark, and American Crow. In 1956, 1959, and 1961, Northern Goshawks fed on a significant number of American Crows. Interestingly enough, most of those crows taken by the Cloquet Goshawks were either nestlings or birds that had recently fledged.

Furthermore, crows were not found nesting closer than three-quarters of a mile from the nesting Northern Goshawks.

Most predators are largely opportunistic, feeding upon the prey species most abundant and easiest to catch. This is why Northern Goshawks have different feeding habits depending on range. In order to create an adequate list of prey species of this large hawk, we need research data from different regions (Storer 1966). For example, in California, Schnell (1958) found that Steller's Jays were an important prey species for a pair of Northern Goshawks, while Eng and Gullion (1962) found that a pair of Northern Goshawks in Minnesota preferred American Crows.

Meng (1959) studied fourteen nesting pairs of Northern Goshawks in Pennsylvania and New York and found American Crows (eighty-three) were the most prevalent prey, followed by red squirrels (fifty-eight). Interestingly enough, they only found five Ruffed Grouse in those nests. Even though the grouse population was high during that period, the gallinaceous birds only comprised a small portion of the Goshawks' diet. Meng studied thirty-four Cooper's Hawks in the same area, at the same time, and found that the most popular prey were European Starlings (241), Northern Flickers (134), and Eastern Meadowlarks (134).

As with Storer (1966), Smithers et al. (2005) found that in Minnesota, mammals were the dominant prey of breeding Northern Goshawks; red squirrels and eastern chipmunks were the two species most delivered to the nests. These two species comprised sixty-two percent of prey identified. The study also indicated that Ruffed Grouse comprised only five percent of prey in Northern Goshawk nests during a three-year period. Interestingly, in Alaska, McGowan (1975) found that snowshoe hares were the primary food source between 1970 and 1972, indicating that Northern Goshawks in some parts of their range don't rely on grouse.

However, there is some conjecture about whether the grouse numbers really are a significant influence on the number of Northern Goshawks produced each year. Throughout much of the west where Northern Goshawks are present, such as Washington, Wyoming, most of Idaho, most of Colorado, all of California, Utah, Nevada, Arizona, and New Mexico, there are no Ruffed Grouse. Therefore, at least, in those states the Ruffed Grouse population cannot be a factor in Northern Goshawk populations.

In Utah, Graham et al. (1999) observed Northern Goshawks preying on animals including snowshoe hares, cottontail rabbits, red, Abert's and flying squirrels, and uinta ground squirrels. The list of birds observed included Northern Flicker, Three-toed Woodpecker, Gray Jay, Black-billed Magpie, American Kestrel, Common Raven, Steller's Jay, American Robin, Townsend's Solitaire, Mourning Dove, Mountain Bluebird, and Mallard.

Of the prey taken by Northern Goshawks in the southwestern United States, according to Reynolds et al. (1992), fourteen species were classified as important, because no single prey species would be numerous enough to support Northern Goshawks, especially during winter and periods of drought. These species include grouse, squirrels, rabbits, woodpeckers, and jays.

Reynolds and Meslow (1984) researching Northern Goshawks in Oregon found snowshoe hares (twenty-four), squirrels (thirteen), along with both golden mantled ground squirrels (seventeen) and northern flying squirrels (fifteen) being the top mammalian species preyed upon by Northern Goshawks that year. As for avian prey, Steller's Jays (twenty-nine), American Robin (twenty) and Northern Flickers (fifteen) topped the list.

The avian prey that impressed me included a single Great Horned Owl, a Northern Saw-whet Owl, and a screech owl. For that matter, I'm always impressed with any bird or animal capable of killing a Great Horned Owl. The Great Horned Owl is truly a formidable predator capable of killing most, if not all, species of North American birds and most medium-sized animals. As for the other smaller owls, they hide so well during the day that it says a lot for the ability for the Northern Goshawk to find them.

American Crows can be an important food source for some Northern Goshawks.

Grouse, like this Dusky Grouse, are a favorite food source of Northern Goshawks.

Every Northern Goshawk nest I've found in Colorado has had Steller's Jay feathers below it.

Large finches nesting at higher elevations, like Pine Grosbeaks, are prey for Northern Goshawks.

A. A. Cross (Bent 1937) documented the following in a Northern Goshawk nest. On May 19 the nest contained the foot of a grouse on the ground below the feathers of a Barred Owl. Five days later, eleven chipmunks and a crow were in the nest uneaten. On June 12 the nest had the remains of two Ruffed Grouse (cleaned to the bone) and a partially eaten chipmunk. The following day there was a single red squirrel in the nest.

In Pennsylvania, during the days when Passenger Pigeons were numerous, Northern Goshawks were considered common; but after the decimation of the pigeons, the hawks were comparatively rare (Bent 1937).

On 12 March 2002, Golet et al. (2003) watched a juvenile Northern Goshawk attack and kill a Wild Turkey in Connecticut. The turkey was feeding under a backyard bird feeder within a small clearing when the hawk struck it. The turkey was apparently unaware of the hawk until the moment of the attack. After a minute the turkey was apparently dead. The hawk fed on the carcass for the next four days.

These hawks have been documented on at least four occasions feeding on carrion when their normal food supply was unavailable (J. Raptor Research, 1995). In 2001, I saw a Rough-Legged Hawk feeding on a dead cow in Wyoming, and I frequently see both Bald and Golden Eagles feeding on road kill, especially along major highways in Wyoming.

Ethier (1999) studying the Queen Charlotte Goshawk and Lewis (2003) studying the Northern Goshawks in southeastern Alaska noted some unusual Goshawk prey including Marbled Murrelets and Pigeon Guillemots.

Shuster (1980) believes that Northern Goshawk populations are highest near large populations of ground squirrels, and, in fact, nests are often within 1,148 feet (350 m) of such an area.

In Oregon, Trailkill et al. (2000) found thirty-nine prey items from two nests, and found that eighty-four percent were birds and sixteen percent were mammals, with Ruffed Grouse comprising forty-five percent of total prey and sixty-four percent of the bird species that were fed upon. The other species consisted of Steller's Jays (thirteen percent), American Robins (thirteen percent), Ring-necked Pheasant (eight percent) and Mountain Quail (five percent). For mammals, he found Douglas squirrel (thirteen percent) and mountain beaver (three percent) being consumed by the hawks.

When hard pressed, Northern Goshawks will forage on dead animals. Squires (1995) observed this phenomenon four times. Three observations were made in the Medicine Bow National Forest in south central Wyoming, when two adult and one bird whose age was not reported were observed feeding on gut piles of mule deer left by hunters. A bird was seen feeding on a gut pile during two consecutive days, but it was uncertain whether it was the same bird both times.

According to Storer (1966), unlike the Cooper's and Sharp-shinned Hawks, it is not surprising that Northern Goshawks prefer animals such as rabbits, hares, and squirrels. Being primarily non-migratory, Northern Goshawks take larger prey during the winter due to a larger energy need. However, there are times when the large hawks make a southward movement, presumably because of a low point in the cycle of their preferred prey.

Numerous researchers have documented the prey of Northern Goshawks. The following list includes virtually all the individual species documented. There are several studies with overlapping prey items, so the unique species are documented singly. Squires and Reynolds (1997) found the hawks preying upon ruffed, dusky, sooty, and Spruce Grouse, blue, Steller's and Gray Jay, American Crow, downy and Hairy Woodpecker, Black-headed Grosbeak, Western Tananger, Pine Grosbeak, Mountain Bluebird, Red Crossbill, Townsend's Solitaire and Williamson's and Red-naped Sapsuckers, and American Robin.

The animals they found the hawks preying upon included tree, ground and flying squirrels, red-backed vole, montane vole, western jumping mouse, American Martin, along with rabbits and hares. Eng and Guillion (1962) found the hawks feeding upon Blue-winged Teal, Common Nighthawk, Pileated Woodpecker, and Eastern Meadowlark. Sutton (1925)

Black-billed Magpies are large, colorful, and slow, making them the perfect prey of Northern Goshawks in the west.

Rabbits and hares are important food sources for Northern Goshawks.

Waterfowl often fall prey to Northern Goshawks in the fall and winter.

found chipmunks, weasels, and white-footed mice. Boals et al. (2006) found that red squirrels made up forty-two percent and eastern chipmunks 19.8 percent of the prey items of Northern Goshawks in the western Great Lakes region. Wood (1938) found Rock Pigeon, domestic fowl, deer mouse, and shrew in the stomachs of hawks in Pennsylvania. Meng (1959) documented American Kestrel, Common Grackle, and Red-winged, Brewer's, and Rusty Blackbirds. Smithers et al. (2005) found American Coot, Green Heron, Cooper's Hawk, Broad-winged Hawk, Northern Goshawk, Barred Owl, Killdeer, Red-breasted Nuthatch, Evening Grosbeak, Ovenbird, Veery, Mallard, and Common Goldeneye. Lewis (2003) documented Northern Goshawks feeding on Pigeon Guillemots in Alaska. He also documented the hawks preying on Varied Thrush; Northwestern Crow; and Willow, Rock, and White-tailed Ptarmigan.

Plucking Posts and Pellets

A plucking post is an area near raptor nests where raptors regularly dismantle their prey before delivering it to their nestlings. The plucking post can be a downed log, a hanging branch, or even a large rock, often elevated. Being elevated from the ground gives the birds a better vantage point to scan for other predators, as they are in a vulnerable state plucking and feeding on their prey.

In Colorado, because of the rocky terrain, Northern Goshawks' plucking posts are most often uphill fifty feet (15.24 m) or more from their nests. In 2011 and 2012 the plucking post that a pair of Northern Goshawks chose was sixty-five feet (19.82 m) uphill from the nest. The post was a sixty-foot (18.29 m) lodgepole pine bowed from base to crown; the center of the tree was about twenty feet (6.10 m) high. Below the tree were feathers from bird species including Steller's Jays, American Robins, and Northern Flickers, as well as fur and bones of Wyoming and golden mantled ground squirrels, mountain cottontails, snowshoe hares, red squirrels, and chipmunks.

Feathers from a Steller's Jay and a Black-billed Magpie found under a Northern Goshawk nest in 2014.

For years, a pair of Northern Goshawks in Rocky Mountain National Park used the bowed lodgepole pine as a plucking post.

Feathers from an American Robin, turkey, and Black-billed Magpie that were found under a Northern Goshawk nest in 2013.

Northern Goshawks used these downed logs as a plucking post in 2012 and 2014.

Eng and Gullion (1962) write about a plucking post they found: "There are several small openings in the forest canopy 100 to 200 feet (30.49–60.98 m) west of the nesting area, partly created by fallen aspen and pines. Several of these trees are broken, the trunks forming horizontal perches two to six feet (.61–1.83 m) above the ground. These perches have been favored by Northern Goshawks for dismembering and devouring their prey, and it has been under these sites that we have found most of the prey remains."

The Northern Goshawk's plucking post is often much farther from the nest than that of either the Cooper's or Sharp-shinned Hawks. In 2006 and 2007, while monitoring a Cooper's Hawk nest on the grounds of the YMCA of the Rockies outside of Estes Park, I located a plucking post that the pair used both years. They chose a downed log a few yards from the nest tree. All around that log were the remains of red squirrels, chipmunks, Clark's Nutcrackers, Steller's Jays, Pine Siskins, House Wrens, and Mourning Doves. Because a female Cooper's Hawk is about the same size as a male Northern Goshawk, they feed on similar types of prey.

A close-up of the plucking post; note the Northern Flicker feathers.

In 1998, I located a Sharp-shinned Hawk nest in Rocky Mountain National Park. After the nesting season was over, I found the plucking post—a downed lodgepole pine a few yards from the nest. Under the tree were the remains of what the family had been feeding upon, including Pine Siskin, House Wren, Yellow-rumped Warbler, Downy Woodpecker, American Robin, and both pygmy and White-breasted Nuthatch.

Hawks, including the Northern Goshawk, cough up or regurgitate pellets. They have a crop, or temporary storage organ, that holds the food. The crop enables the birds to gorge themselves when they have the opportunity, as they may go several hours or even days between meals. Swallowing large amounts of food rapidly and then storing it helps the birds to eat quickly and then fly to cover.

Hawks regurgitate the pellets with a vomiting motion, jerking forward and backward slightly and leaning down as the pellet falls to the ground. Northern Goshawk pellets are often comprised of feathers and fur with few, if any, bones.

Northern Goshawk pellets and a quarter for size comparison.

A dissected Northern Goshawk pellet, with a quarter for comparison.

Chapter Three

Nest Characteristics

Between 2005 and 2014, I located fifteen active Northern Goshawk nests in and around RMNP. Eight were in quaking aspen, three were in ponderosa pine, three were in a lodgepole pine, and one was in a Douglas fir. All nests were above 8,000 feet (2,438 m) and within a few yards of an active water source, such as a creek, stream, or lake. All but two nests were in a wooded area comprised primarily of ponderosa pine, quaking aspen, and spruce. The two oddball nests were in a lodgepole pine stand. All nests had a significant number of downed logs around them.

In 2010 and 2014, I located nests in a lodgepole pine forest. The forest within 150 yards (137 m) of these nests was comprised entirely of lodgepole pine and juniper. However, south of the nests, the forest consisted of aspen and ponderosa with tall (more than three feet (0.91 m) high) grasses. To the east was mostly spruce-fir forest. In 2014, a nest was several feet from the trunk of the dead tree, with no live vegetation above the nest. However, there were a few dead lodgepole pine needles and pine cones above it.

In 2011, I was fortunate to locate two Northern Goshawk nests, one in a live aspen and the other in a dead Douglas fir. The nest in the aspen was just a few inches from an active hiking trail inside the park. The female hawk attacked anyone who came near. Interestingly enough, she didn't attack people on horseback; she would just cackle from a distance. That nest was relatively low, about thirty feet (9.14 m) off the ground. Above the nest were several live aspen branches with leaves that seemed to camouflage it from above and shade the young while the adults were foraging.

The second nest was in a 100-foot (30.5 m) tall dead Douglas fir. The nest was a little more than halfway up the tree. This was obviously used by Northern Goshawks in the past because it was over four feet (4.27 m) in diameter and almost three feet (.91 m) deep. As with the other nests I've come across, this one was against the trunk of the tree. (The other nests that I found which were built that same year were smaller, roughly two feet [61.5 cm] wide and two feet [61.5 cm] deep). The branches above that nest were covered with dead fir needles. The area around that nest consisted of lodgepole pine, fir, aspen, spruce, and ground junipers. This was the first nest I had seen in a dead tree and so far from a trail or logging road. However, the nest was only eighty yards (24.39 m) from a meadow. Furthermore, eighty percent of the trees around that nest were dead, and there were hundreds of downed logs in the area as well. There were so many downed logs that I was convinced no animal except squirrels would be able to get near the nest. It was even difficult to hike there.

All but one of the nests I've observed were built against the trunk of a tree, and five were within 150 yards (137 m) of a hiking or horse trail. Three nest trees were within inches of horse trails. All nests were within a quarter mile of a lake or stream. Two nests were within view of an active stream. My theory about why birds nest near trails is that it is easier for the males to find their way back from hunting. However, it is also possible that more nests are found near trails because that's where the are the most visible to people looking for them. Each nest site was close to large trees (more than thirty feet (9.15 m)

A Northern Goshawk nest at Deer Ridge Junction in Rocky Mountain National Park.

high) that had little understory vegetation. All the nest trees had downed logs nearby and were on a slope that varied from ten percent to thirty percent. Five of the nests were 400 yards (366 m) or less from large openings in the forest. These openings ranged from a few acres to a half mile (2,023.4 m²) or more in size. This could be one of the reasons that the hawks feed heavily on Wyoming ground squirrels and golden mantled ground squirrels. The golden mantled ground squirrels reside in the forests and the Wyoming ground squirrels are found in the adjacent meadows.

A Northern Goshawk nesting area is approximately thirty acres (12.49 ha) and may include up to eight different nests (Squires and Reynolds, 1997). The home range, including the nest area, post-fledging area, and foraging area, can be as large as 6,000 acres (2,428 ha) (Reynolds et al., 1992).

In 2012, I found three Northern Goshawk nests. One nest was in a dead spruce inside RMNP that a pair of hawks had used in 2011. I believe they also used it the following year. Unfortunately, on June 20, 2012, I found that nest on the ground under the tree. It had apparently blown out a few days earlier. Among the branches were adult Northern Goshawk feathers and eggshell fragments, but no remains of adults or nestlings.

A second nest found that year had also failed. It was in a live aspen in RMNP up the trail from a large pond called the East Portal, just outside the YMCA of the Rockies. The nest was very close to a hiking trail, which may be the reason why it failed. Often, if the female can't handle the stress of people near her nest during incubation, she will abandon her nest. No adults were found near that nest as of June 7.

Typical Northern Goshawk nest in an aspen tree in Rocky Mountain National Park.

This Northern Goshawk nest is in a lodgepole pine forest. The nest is in the center of the photo.

I located a third active nest that year. These Northern Goshawks chose to nest in RMNP in the same aspen that they had used in 2010. In 2012 the pair began raising three young hawks, but shortly after June 20, only two nestlings remained. The third nestling was never found.

Shuster (1980) found Northern Goshawk nests in the Arapaho and Roosevelt National Forests and RMNP in similar environments. From 1971 through 1977, he located twenty nests; ten were in aspen, five in ponderosa pine, and five in lodgepole pine. Trees housing the nests were between forty-five and seventy-nine feet (13.7 to 24.1 m) tall; the average was sixty-three feet (19.2 m) tall. He also found that the preferred nesting tree was the quaking aspen. All nests were in living trees, and all but two were nestled against the trunk. The slope of the nest sites varied from zero to forty percent, with the average being 12.5 percent. Most nests were on a gentle slope with a north or east aspect. All of them had a 0.1-acre (0.4 ha.) or larger opening within 1,148 feet (350 m). Shuster also noted that the preferred prey in his study areas were Wyoming ground squirrels and golden mantled ground squirrels. He also surmised that the hawks chose these sites due to the abundance of ground squirrels. In addition, he found that the hawks built their nests within about 900 yards (823 m) of water.

Speiser and Bosakowski (1987) found that in northern New Jersey and southeastern New York, there was no significant slope to the nest sites that Northern Goshawks chose. However, they were generally found on lower, gentle slopes and flat areas. The hawks seemed to avoid south-facing slopes. Notably, the nest sites found during the study were closer to swamps than they were to lakes or streams.

In 2010, a pair of Northern Goshawks nested in the Upper Beaver Meadows area of RMNP, in a live aspen approximately thirty-three feet high (10.06 m). The nest itself was a little more than twenty-three feet (7.01 m) from the ground. Above the nest were branches and leaves that shaded the young. I remember being at the nest on June 29 and seeing the female perched on one foot next to the nest. She was fully shaded as she monitored her surroundings. That nest was made entirely of sticks and measured approximately 6.5 feet (1.98 m) across and three feet (.91 m) deep.

With the exception of the nest in the dead fir in 2011 and the nest in a dead lodgepole in 2014, every accipiter nest that I have ever located was in a live tree that had a canopy of vegetation (pine needles or leaves). Shuster (1980) found that lives trees were a deciding factor in determining a nest tree. The Sharp-shined Hawk nest I found in 1998 was in a live Douglas fir, and all of the Cooper's Hawk nests that I have found over the years were in lodgepole pine, aspen, or ponderosa pine. All of the Cooper's Hawk nests were smaller than Northern Goshawk nests, and the Sharp-Shinned hawk nest was smaller than the Cooper's Hawk nests.

In 2009, a pair of Northern Goshawks built their nest in a live lodgepole pine. The nest was against the trunk of the tree a little more than thirty feet (8.42 m) from the ground, roughly three feet (0.91 m) across, and built of sticks. The tree was thirteen feet (3.42 m) from a horse trail that had been used for many summers and was going to be used again that season. For the safety of the birds and horseback riders, I explained to the barn manager that the hawks can be quite aggressive when anyone approaches their nest, and he rerouted the trail.

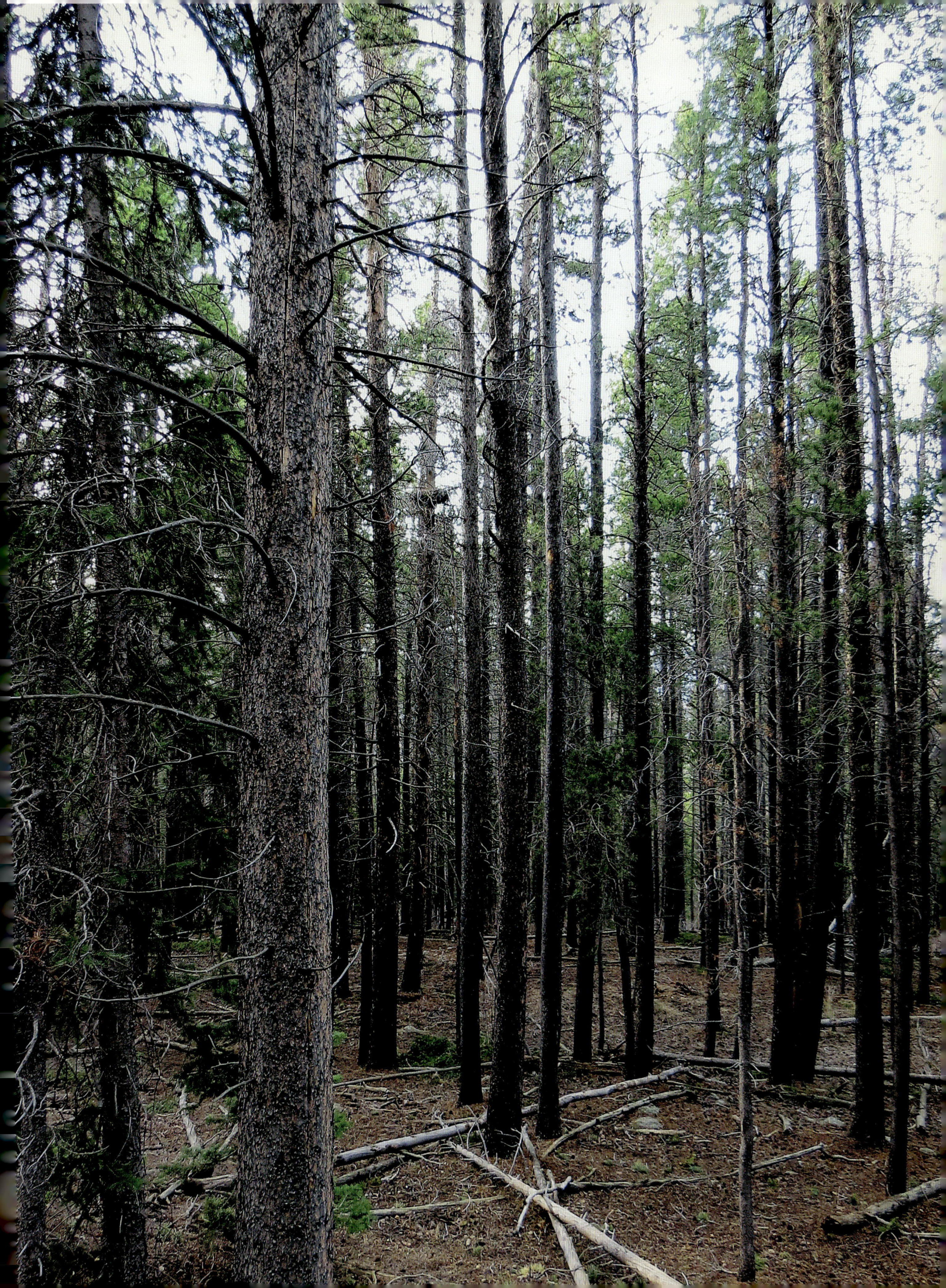

Sometime Northern Goshawks build their nests along trails used by people.

Northern Goshawk nest along the Storm Pass Trail in Rocky Mountain National Park.

An atypical Northern Goshawk nest; normally Northern Goshawks construct their nests against the tree trunk.

42

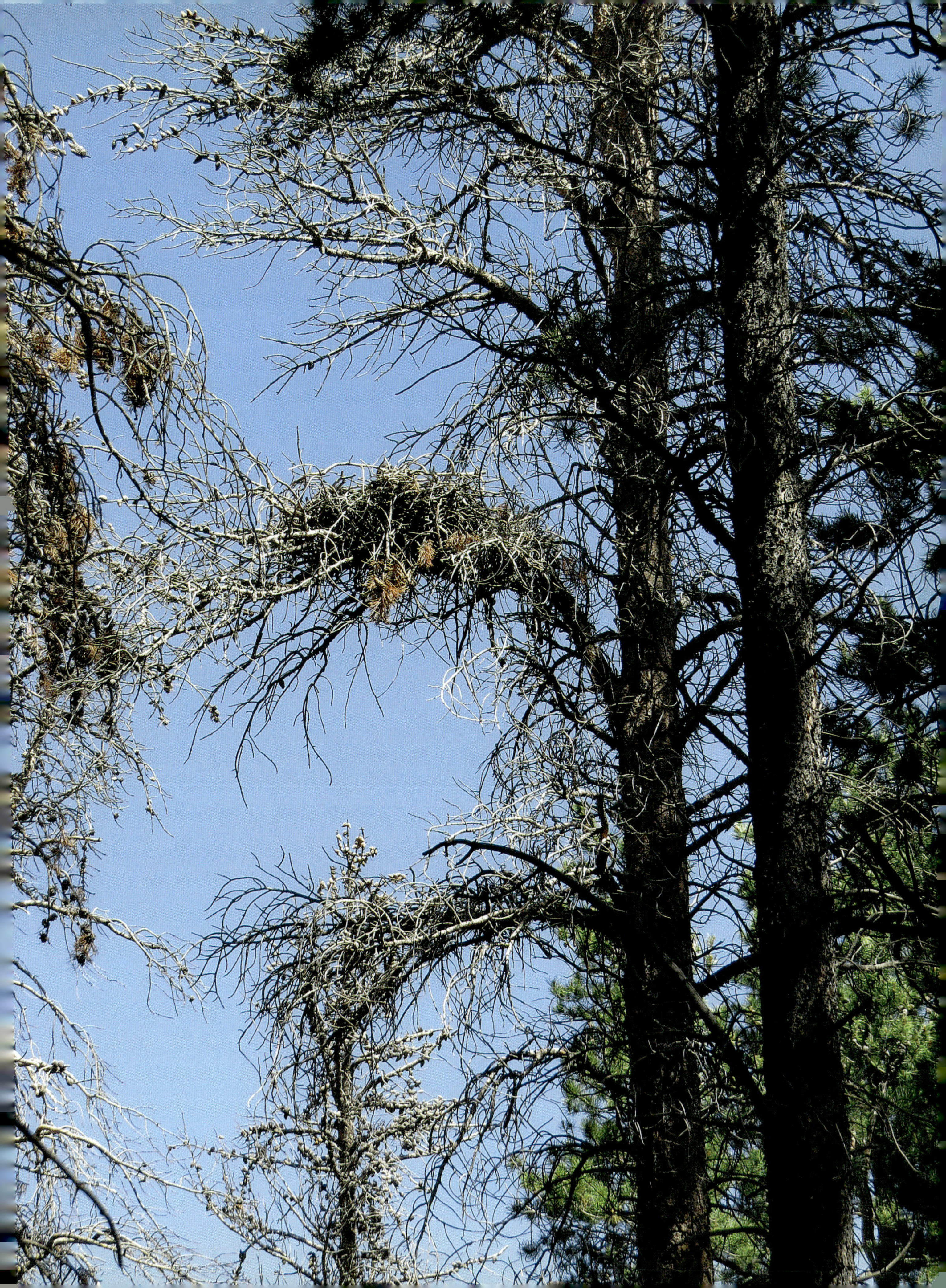

Adult female Northern Goshawk perched next to her nest in 2012.

A female Northern Goshawk incubating her eggs.

Adult female Northern Goshawk perched on her nest next to her day-old young hawk, not visible in this photo.

Adult female Northern Goshawk perched on her nest with one of her week-old youngsters.

45

I monitored the adults and young from incubation through fledging, and to my astonishment, was not attacked a single time. That was a first for me.

That nest tree was on a north-facing slope and, with the exception of a handful of juniper, all of the trees within forty feet (3.72 m) were lodgepole pines. To the north and west were two small creeks with aspen and a few ponderosas. The area downslope from the nest was made up primarily of ponderosa and aspen, with lodgepole and spruce upslope.

In 1935, Gromme described a Northern Goshawk nest as bulky and resting in a crotch against the main trunk of a large live Yellow Birch. It was about thirty-five feet from the ground, and the tree trunk at the nest measured about fourteen inches at the diameter.

Gromme goes on to say: "The nest was a substantially built affair, measuring approximately six feet to the extremities of the outer straggling branches used in its construction, the largest of which were not over a half inch in diameter. It was neatly and evenly cupped and lined with smaller twigs. Around its edge and facing inward were a few small, green balsam sprigs which lent an appearance of artistry and color. The interior of the nest was as neat as a pin and excrement was evidently ejected over the edge as very little appeared on the rim. The ground and foliage below were considerably whitewashed."

According to Speiser and Bosakowski (1991) most Northern Goshawks in New York and New Jersey are probably permanent residents. Most of the breeding birds begin regular visits to their nest sites in late February and begin adding fresh nesting material by mid-March. Nest sites were being used and reused for up to eight years.

In contrast, they did not find Cooper's or Sharp-shinned Hawks reusing the same nest in consecutive years. However, in 2005 and 2006, I found a pair of Cooper's Hawks nesting at the YMCA of the Rockies that used the same nest for two consecutive years. That nest was in a ponderosa pine less than six feet (1.83 m) from a hiking trail. Five years was the longest that Reynolds and Wight found Northern Goshawks using the same nest, though not consecutively. On the other hand, they found a pair of Cooper's Hawks using a nest for three years and a Sharp-Shinned Hawk using a nest for two years; again, not consecutively.

Major Bendire (1892) in Bent (1937) found several Northern Goshawk nests. One was in a large cottonwood tree about fifty feet (15.24 m) off the ground. "It was a bulky affair, fully measuring two feet in diameter and quite as deep. The nest was composed of sticks, some of them quite large and loosely put together. It was rather shallow on top and lined with weed stalks, a species of wild nettle, and a few pine needles."

Bendire describes another nest that was on the top of a juniper tree twenty feet (6.10 m) from the ground. It was placed inside the juniper and apparently well-hidden. On April 18, 1876, the eggs were already being incubated. Another nest was found on April 9, 1877, in a tall pine at least fifty feet (15.24 m) from the ground.

All nest sites were in areas with little undergrowth, which is an obvious decision-maker for nest placement. The reason for this is not fully understood, but I am going to take a crack at it.

Nests in live trees are camouflaged from above, so they are not detected by passing birds, such as crows and ravens, that could harm the eggs and young. Furthermore, when the young fledge, ample branches on the nearby trees allow them to make short flights and strengthen their muscles. And a clear understory gives the hawks full view of any predators coming from below, and a clear line of attack.

Bent (1937) notes that of the sixty-two Northern Goshawk nests he documented, only eleven were in conifers, including seven in white pines, two in firs, one in a spruce, and

An active Northern Goshawk nest; notice the canopy of green leaves above the nest.

Adult female Northern Goshawk perched in the woods. You can see that the bird is molting. Old feathers are brown, new feathers are blue-gray.

Adult Northern Goshawks molt during the nesting season. Their feathers can often be found on the ground around their nest tree.

one in a hemlock. As for the rest of the nests, eighteen were in beech, fourteen in birch, eleven in poplar, six in maple, and there were single nests in an oak and cottonwood. Turner (1886) (in Bent 1937) claims the species has nested on cliffs in Alaska.

Northern Goshawks often build several nests in their territory. The unused nests are perfect places for other species to set up housekeeping. Because Great Horned Owls nest earlier in the spring than Northern Goshawks do, Kennedy (2003) found Great Horned Owls will use the nests of Northern Goshawks to raise their family. In one case, a Great Horned Owl moved into a Northern Goshawk nest, and the hawks rebuilt a new nest a few hundred yards away.

Great Gray Owls and Cooper's Hawks will use Northern Goshawk nests, too. Bull et al. (1988) found Great Grays using the nests in Oregon. Great Gray Owls also use the nests of Common Ravens and Red-tailed Hawks.

Eggs and Incubation

Northern Goshawks usually lay two to five pale blue to light blue eggs. "These are ovate to elliptical-oval or oval in shape. The shell is rather rough, finely granulated or pitted" (Bent 1937). The eggs measure, on average, 59.2 mm by 45.1 mm, with the largest being 65.5 mm by 47.3 mm and the smallest 52.7 mm by 43.9 mm (Bent 1937). Northern Goshawks lay one egg every two to three days and appear to begin incubating with the first egg laid. The female incubates with exclusivity (Reynolds and Wight 1978). Eighty percent of Northern Goshawks begin incubating during the second through fourth weeks of April; the average onset of incubation is April 23 (Speiser and Bosakowski 1991). Reynolds and Wight (1978) found the earliest completed clutch appeared on April 10 and the latest

For two nesting seasons, this female Northern Goshawk would perch low in the woods near her nest.

Adult female Northern Goshawks are almost always in view of their nest and young.

on June 2. Most clutches were completed and incubation was underway by the last week in April.

According to Reynolds and Wight (1978), in Oregon, incubation for all three accipiters seems to be between thirty and thirty-two days. However, Bent (1937) lists Northern Goshawk incubation at twenty-eight days, Cooper's Hawk incubation at twenty-four days, and Sharp-shinned Hawk incubation at twenty-one to twenty-four days. I did observe a nesting pair of Cooper's Hawk whose eggs hatched after being incubated for thirty-five days.

In North America, Squires and Reynolds (1997) have suggested that a canopy that is at least eight-two percent closed is one of the most common habitat aspects of Northern Goshawk nest sites. After the young have hatched, the female will carry the eggshells away from the nest and drop them in the forest. Sometimes the eggshells will be light blue to almost white, due to the color wearing off the eggshell. I have found both egg colors near Northern Goshawk nests.

Nesting and Nest Defense

Northern Goshawks occupy nest areas from March through September (Reynolds et al., 1992) with both male and female participating in nest construction and repair (Iverson et al., 1996). In Oregon, Northern Goshawks appeared at their nests in late March and early April (Reynolds and Meslow, 1984).

On June 1, 2010, I located an active Northern Goshawk nest in a live aspen within RMNP. It looked like it had been constructed some years earlier because it seemed to be in disrepair. As I approached, I saw the tail of the incubating female extending over one side. Assuming incubation was still under way, I decided to leave and return in a day or so. As I walked away, I heard tapping coming from an aspen a few yards from the hawk nest. There I found a male Three-toed Woodpecker constructing its nest.

Throughout incubation, the Goshawk nest was devoid of greenery. It wasn't until after the young hatched that I noticed some live spruce boughs and aspen branches on the nest. The birds may have added them for camouflage.

On day fifteen I arrived at 1:00 p.m. and noticed that there was a horse trail a few yards from the nest. While I was monitoring the surroundings, several people on horseback rode along the trail fifty yards (15.24 m) from the hawk's nest.

I'm sure the female Northern Goshawk noticed the horses, but she didn't appear to care, as she perched motionless. The nest tree was at an elevation of 8,860 feet (2,701 m) and the nest was about thirty feet (9.14 m) from the ground. Evidently, the distance from the horse trail to her nest was far enough that the horseback riders did not bother her.

I returned on June 29 and saw two, two-and a-half week-old chicks about the size of a young chicken. At first I didn't notice the female, so I assumed she was out hunting. After setting up my camera, I began scanning the area and found the female perched on the limb of a live aspen twenty feet (6.10 m) south. She was so content that she never moved, and at times even perched on one foot. I stayed for almost an hour.

A bird perched on one foot is usually a sign of contentment. Occasionally, though, a bird may perch on one foot if the other foot or leg is injured. This bird was not injured; she was just unconcerned about our presence.

Colorado was extremely dry that summer and a fire broke out on the north side of RMNP several miles from the hawk nest. The fire fighters needed to close the road and trail near the nest so that the helicopters could use the helipad to pick up and drop off

An adult male Northern Goshawk perched near his nest.

A Northern Goshawk eggshell next to a molted feather.

A female Northern Goshawk on her nest in a dead spruce. This nest was used for several years before it was found on the ground under the tree.

firefighters. After some communication with the Park Service and fire fighters, I was able to get into the area to continue my research. This turned out to be the best thing for the birds because it ensured that no one could hike near the nest.

By early July, the female was leaving the young hawks alone and spending more time hunting. On July 6, I arrived at the nest at 3:00 p.m. and could hear the food-begging calls of the two nestling Three-toed Woodpeckers nearby. Not seeing the female Northern Goshawk in the area, I walked to the woodpecker nest to get a few photos. While I was photographing, I wondered, "Why hasn't the female Northern Goshawk taken these woodpeckers?" To this day, I can't understand why she spared those birds. Northern Goshawks have been documented killing Three-toed Woodpeckers (Graham et al., 1999). I made my way back to an area where I had a clear view of the nest, enabling me to get some photos of the hawk's nest. Then, a little after 3:30 p.m., she landed on the nest with a red squirrel clenched in her left foot. (Northern Goshawks enter their nests from below the canopy, whereas Buteos such as Red-tailed Hawks enter their nests from above because they place their nests on the tops of trees (Squires and Kennedy). Both young hawks moved toward her, twittering. The female began tearing small pieces of flesh from the squirrel and fed it to the young. It seemed as if the nestlings were taking turns taking the bits of meat from their mom. After a few minutes, the young birds appeared to be full. The adult female looked around for a few moments; then she flew off with what was left of the squirrel.

According to McClaren et al. (2005), the nesting period of Northern Goshawks is roughly forty days, give or take 1.3 days. Reynolds and Wight (1978), on the other hand, stated that the time young hawks remain on the nest is thirty-four to thirty-seven days, which coincides with my observations. The birds fledged sometime between July 16 and 19. If my calculations were correct, the Northern Goshawk nestlings were in their nest for thirty-seven days.

The nest was empty when I returned on July 19, and the hawks were nowhere to be found. I searched the area for several minutes when I heard an adult Northern Goshawk calling east of the nest. I moved through the woods a few hundred yards until I spotted the male, perched on the limb of a lodgepole with a partially eaten squirrel clenched in his right foot. He was giving a call that I had not previously heard—a series of two to seven short crow-like cackles, apparently to let the female know he had food for her.

That same year, I found that a pair of Northern Goshawks (presumably the same pair) had returned to the same nest in an aspen that they had occupied two years previously. I showed my photographer friend John and his wife the nest so that he could get some good photos. He has a 500 mm lens for his cameras, and I had only a 300 mm lens. After seeing the nest, he asked if he could bring a friend. I said yes but asked them to stay together and move as a unit. Northern Goshawks don't seem capable of comprehending more than one or two things happening at a time. The following day, I returned to the hawk nest to continue monitoring the nesting cycle. As I approached, the female was perched on the nest with her two youngsters, feeding them a squirrel.

For the first time during that season and the previous one, she dropped off her nest and began cackling as she flew over my head carrying the squirrel. In the blink of an eye, she returned, landing several yards from the nest. I walked toward her to see if I could get a few photos. She obviously knew I was around so trying to hide was futile. As she was scolding me, I noticed her under-tail coverts were flaring and assumed it was a sign of agitation.

Interestingly, this female cackled at me only when I was looking at her. After I took a few photos, I began talking to her, explaining that I was not going to hurt her or her kids. I also told her that it isn't fair to attack someone who is trying to leave. As I walked away, I heard a swooshing sound and turned around to see that she was within a few feet and aiming for my head. She swerved and landed in an aspen above me. I made my way down toward the trail leading to my car. She continued her onslaught even when I was

Nestling Northern Goshawks.

A Northern Goshawk chick, just a few days old; if you look closely, you can see the egg tooth on the upper mandible. *Photo by Wayne Johnston*

A male Three-toed Woodpecker at his nest just a few feet from an active Northern Goshawk nest.

A female Three-toed Woodpecker at her nest with one of her nestlings visible.

A female Northern Goshawk on her nest in 2014, calling to her mate to bring food.

Adult female Northern Goshawk screaming at me, a few days after several people approached her nest.

over fifty yards (45.50 m) from her nest. At that point she landed in an aspen where another pair of Three-toed Woodpeckers were nesting. Shortly after, she flew back to her nest. According to Speiser and Bosakowski (1991), females defend their nests more aggressively than males. This certainly seems to be the case, as I had not been attacked by the male of that pair.

The reason for the attack soon became clear. Unbeknownst to me, a few days earlier, John had brought three other people with him. In the beginning, they all stayed together and watched the nest. But as John lingered to photograph the female on her nest, his friends walked in different directions to search for the plucking post. With four people moving randomly around her, she apparently sensed danger.

In 2012, the third nest that I found was also used by a pair of hawks in 2010. Those young hawks had hatched on or about May 28, 2012. On June 20, I photographed three young in the nest. But when I returned eight days later, only two young remained. I don't know if the third one died, fell out of the nest, or was eaten by its nest mates. Those two young hawks began branching in early July and had fledged around July 10. The parents had fed their young ground squirrels, snowshoe hares, and a few birds including Northern Flickers, Clark's Nutcrackers, and American Robins.

In 2014, the pair (or at least a pair) of Northern Goshawks used that same nest again. Apparently they have two nests within their territory and use one nest every other year. On May 1, I found both male and female Northern Goshawks near the nest, and on May 7 the female was incubating. The first egg hatched about June 14 and the young fledged on July 16.

Adult female Northern Goshawk cackling near her nest.

An angry Northern Goshawk; note the flaring white under-tail coverts.

Clark's Nutcrackers are often taken as prey by Northern Goshawks in the west.

American Robins are a staple of the Northern Goshawk diet throughout North America.

These images show an attack by a female Northern Goshawk.

    I arrived at the nest site just after sunrise that morning to find the two young still on the nest. The first young hawk began walking on the branches near the nest, then at a few minutes after 6:00 a.m. it took a short flight, about six feet (1.83 m), to the nearby ponderosa and looked around for over half an hour. As I watched, the second youngster took its first flight, albeit a short one, at 7:15 a.m.

    In spring 2011, the National Park Service began receiving reports of a large hawk that was swooping at hikers along the Storm Pass Trail. Jeff Connor, a national park employee, had previously seen the nest and been attacked by the female. "When you get near the nest, you'll know it," he said. The trail was carved through aspen, spruce, and lodgepole pine and crossed Glacier Creek. On June 29, I went to see the Storm Pass nest. Before I could find it, I heard the familiar *kak-kak-kak-kak-kak* as the adult female approached me. I quickly located the nest in a live aspen; the two young hawks inside appeared to be roughly two weeks old. They were covered in white down, and I could see tiny primary wing feathers. A short time later, I heard the deeper *kak- kak-kak-kak-kak* of the male. He flew at me with a lifeless golden mantled ground squirrel clutched in one foot.

    As he passed over, I heard a soft thump behind me. I turned around to find the dead squirrel on the ground. The hawk had dropped it near me as a fighter pilot would drop a bomb on its intended target. I moved a few yards away to photograph the young and then went back the same way I had come. The squirrel was gone! The male had evidently swooped back and picked it up. I did not see him deliver it to the female, but I presume he stored it somewhere close by to be delivered after I left.

Three Northern Goshawk nestlings are an unusual sight within Rocky Mountain National Park. Shortly after this photo was taken, only two nestlings remained.

It is common for Northern Goshawks around Rocky Mountain National Park to raise two young. Note the fresh spruce bows on the nest.

A nestling and its sibling at the Beaver Meadows nest in Rocky Mountain National Park. This photo was taken on July 16, 2014, just after 6:00 a.m.

A snowshoe hare foot found at a plucking post.

The nestling from the Beaver Meadow nest taken on July 16, 2014, a short time before it fledged.

A fledgling Northern Goshawk, minutes after leaving its nest for the first time.

Northern Goshawk nestlings from Storm Pass Trail, photographed on June 29, 2011.

I returned weekly to document the hawks' growth. On several occasions, horseback riders moved directly under the nest. The female would cackle but not attack. However, every time I watched hikers pass under the nest, the female would swoop at them, cackling as they passed. The first young hawk fledged July 12, and the second took the plunge three days later.

On June 1, 2009, Estes Park resident Ed Weisner was hiking along a horse trail at a youth camp outside Estes Park when he came upon a large nest in a lodgepole pine next to the trail. He also saw a Northern Goshawk fly through the woods past him.

Knowing that I am interested in birds of prey, he called me to describe what he had found. The next day I hiked to the location he described. I found the nest and saw a second-year female Cooper's Hawk fly through the woods. I told Ed what I had found; he was convinced that he saw a Northern Goshawk, and I was convinced that I saw a Cooper's Hawk. Now we had a dilemma. Which species was using that nest?

We made plans to return together on June 5. What we found was the tail of a Northern Goshawk hanging over a nest constructed in a live lodgepole pine about twenty feet (6.10 m) from the ground. Question answered. The nest was about six feet (1.83 m) in diameter and three feet (.91 m) deep. It had been placed against the trunk of the tree. The pine branches below the nest were mostly dead, whereas the branches above the nest were still alive with lots of green needles. As a matter of fact, all the trees in the immediate vicinity were live, and the forest was so dense that there wasn't enough sunlight hitting the forest floor to enable much vegetation to grow. Therefore, there really wasn't much on the forest floor except pine needles, rocks, and a few downed logs. The lack of understory may help adult birds to see mammalian predators approaching.

Like the other nests I've located, there was no greenery around the top of this nest until after the eggs had hatched. The adult hawk, presumably the female, placed live aspen branches on the nest, apparently to conceal it. The young hatched on or about 7 June, because on that day, I found a light blue eggshell on the ground a few yards from the nest. I also found a Cooper's Hawk feather, suggesting that maybe the Cooper's Hawk became a meal for the larger accipiter. Unlike the other Northern Goshawk nests that I've monitored, this female never tried to attack me or my photographer friends throughout the entire nesting season. This was a first for me.

In 2014, a pair of Northern Goshawks constructed a nest just a few yards from the afore-mentioned nest. This nest, however, was atypical in several ways. First, it was constructed in a dead lodgepole pine. Second, the nest was about four feet (1.22 m) from the trunk of the tree. Also, it appeared that the male hawk had been killed because on several visits, the nestling was alone. Normally the female is always within sight of the nest (as long as the male keeps delivering food). The adult female was likely the sole provider for her single chick. This may have been why there was just one; she could not find enough food for more.

The young bird fledged at 10:08 a.m. on July 23. As it began taking short flights to adjacent trees, the mother flew off. The young hawk found a comfortable lodgepole limb to perch on. After taking several photos of the young hawk, I made my way under the nest to search for prey remains. There I spotted the remains of a Black-billed Magpie, Northern Flicker, and Steller's Jay, proving that the single mother was a good provider.

After moving to Colorado in 1998, I worked at a resort that had a livery stable. One afternoon, the barn manager told me of a large hawk that would routinely attack hikers and horseback riders that ventured down a particular trail. I hiked to the area that he

A female Northern Goshawk taking flight as its mate comes near its nest.

A juvenile Cooper's Hawk.

described, and before I got within a hundred yards of the nest, I heard the familiar *cak-cak-cak-cak-cak* of a Northern Goshawk. Her nest was in a live aspen about twenty-five feet (7.62 m) from the ground and roughly three feet (0.91 m) from the top of the tree. The nest was against the trunk, and the tree itself was a few feet from the horse trail. The pair raised three young that year. A pair of Northern Goshawks used that same nest again (probably the same pair, though there were no markings that let me know for sure) in 2004 and raised two young as well. They fed on a significant number of Gray Jays, red squirrels, and golden-mantled ground squirrels.

I found intriguing the sheer number of small mammals living close to the nest tree, including chipmunks and red squirrels. I wondered if the hawks were saving them for their offspring to try out their hunting prowess. Unfortunately, I was not around to validate that hypothesis.

I knew that the barn manager would often shoot creatures that caused problems around the barn, including magpies and crows. I asked him why he hadn't killed that hawk. He replied that the hawk virtually depleted the magpie and crow populations.

The female's tail protruding from the edge of the nest is often the only visible clue that the nest is active.

A Northern Goshawk nest in a lodgepole pine forest.

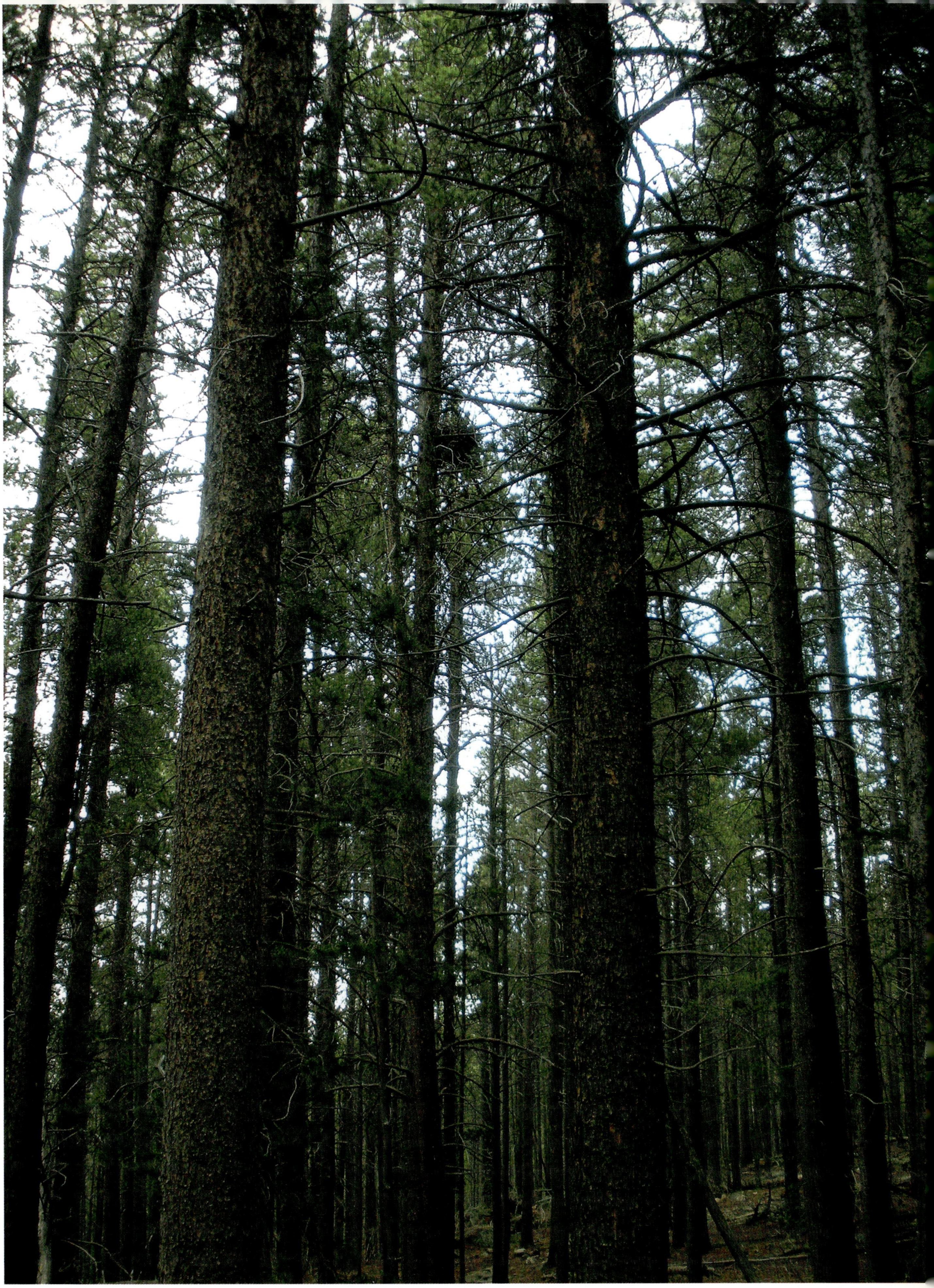

This is an atypical Northern Goshawk nest, since it is not against the tree trunk.

    The following year, I was told about a large hawk that had constructed a nest in RMNP—oddly, about a mile (1.60 km) north of the afore-mentioned nest. Again, the park employee said, "When you get close, you'll know it." Sure enough, as I approached, I heard the familiar *cak-cak-cak-cak-cak* of a Northern Goshawk. A few seconds later an adult hawk flew at my head and landed on a pine branch behind me. I walked in the direction the bird came from and found a bushel-size nest about twenty-five feet (7.62 m) off the ground in a live lodgepole pine. The nest had two young hawks dressed in the familiar sepia-colored juvenile plumage. Both birds were perched erect, watching me and their mother. The nest tree was about 1,200 yards (1,097 m) east of Highway 7, 250 yards (229 m) from a logging road that cut through the woods and about 1,500 yards (1,372 m) from Lily Lake.
    This aggressive female cackled at and attacked anything that came within view of her nest, including deer, elk, and people. The only living things I saw near her nest that year were Ruby-crowned Kinglets gleaning insects from the pine needles. They were likely too small to warrant her attention.
    The young hawks fledged on July 12 and spent the next few days making short flights through the trees. It was interesting to watch the interaction between the young hawks and the Gray Jays that harassed them when their parents were not around. The jays seemed to have a scout that would keep an eye open for the adults' return. I always knew when the adult birds were on their way back because the jays would call out and instantly fly away.

Nestling Northern Goshawks photographed on June 30.

Small songbirds, like Mountain Chickadees and House Wrens, often nest near large raptors like goshawks, knowing that the hawk will keep predators away from their nests.

It took only three days for the young hawks to become proficient fliers. On one of the last visits, I found a raccoon literally in pieces. Parts of the animal extended in every direction for about eight feet (2.44 m), with the torso partially buried. Around the body parts were the tracks of at least two mountain lions, one larger than the other, most likely a mother and kitten.

Of all of the accipiter nests that I've come across, I've never found another accipiter nesting anywhere nearby. However, in Oregon, Reynolds and Wight (1978) found a Sharp-shinned Hawk's nest approximately 1,470 yards (1,344 m) from an active Northern Goshawk nest and five Cooper's Hawk nests within 980 yards (896 m) and 1,476 yards (1,350 m) of active Northern Goshawk nests. There are several accounts where the larger accipiters have preyed upon the smaller. So nesting too close to one another can be detrimental.

Most of the Northern Goshawk nests that Speiser and Bosakowski (1987) found in northern New Jersey and southeastern New York were built in deciduous hardwood trees rather than conifers; American beech and black birch were used more frequently than the authors expected because there were fewer hardwoods than conifers in the nesting areas. All of the trees used for nesting were live and generally large in diameter, and the nest height averaged 39.4 feet (12 m) from the ground. They, too, found several nests within close proximity to trails or roads within the woods, suggesting that the birds use these roads and trails as lanes for hunting. Speiser and Bosakowski believe that these roads or trails serve as landmarks or reference points for their nests.

McClaren et al. (2005) found that the median hatching date for Northern Goshawks in New Mexico was May 29 (N=17), the median fledging date was July 7 (N=17), and the median date when the birds left their post-fledging area (PFA) was August 25 (N=15).

A single Northern Goshawk nestling, photographed on July 18, 2014.

The same bird, photographed on July 23, 2014, the day it fledged.

It took the bird a few tries to find a comfortable place to perch.

Trails near Northern Goshawk nests may help the birds relocate their nest after returning from a hunting foray.

Nestlings

Boals (1994) and Bent (1937) describe the growth of young Northern Goshawks as follows. At hatching, chicks are about 13 cm (5 1/8 inch) in length, covered above with soft white to light grayish downy feathers, yet their undersides have few feathers. They lay horizontally and mostly out of view below the nest edge. Depending on the depth of the nest, their heads can be visible. The little ones may give whistle-like food-begging calls while being fed. Starting at about five days of age, the young can defecate over the edge of the nest. The female broods nestlings during the day (when needed) and after dark and until they are between nine and fourteen days old (Boals, 1994).

In 2010, I located a Northern Goshawk nest inside RMNP that contained two young. I suspected that the first egg hatched around June 10. In 2011, I located two nests inside RMNP. The eggs from one nest hatched about June 15, while the eggs from the other nest hatched about July 1.

On June 15, the female was perched on an aspen branch a few feet from the nest. The young were little white balls of fluff, barely able to keep their heads up. Occasionally one would raise its head high enough to be briefly visible above the edge of the nest. Their small size suggested that they had hatched on the tenth. After the young hatch, the female will brood them from sun and weather. That year, it was quite warm, and the live aspen was shady enough to keep the nestlings comfortable.

A Northern Goshawk nestling about seventeen days after hatching.

On June 30, the young hawks were about the size of a chicken. Their mostly white heads had some brown juvenile feathers visible just above and behind the eyes. There were also brown feathers on their wings and flanks. By July 3, the young hawks were almost entirely covered with juvenile plumage; their tails were about four inches long with a pale terminal band. The young hawks were constantly aware of their surroundings; the slightest noise often brought them to attention.

Boals (1994) writes that from hatching through fledging and even several days after, young birds spend a lot of their time lying down, a term called sternal recumbency. Presumably, their legs aren't strong enough for them to perch for long periods.

From nine to twelve days after hatching, the young are roughly 6–7$^{1}/_{8}$ inches (15–18 cm) long. They spend most of their time lying in the bowl of the nest out of view. They move mostly to be fed and defecate over the edge. Being fed helps them acquire good head movement, yet they are unable to balance and often use their wings to do so.

At fourteen to seventeen days old, they are 8–9$^{1}/_{8}$ inches (20–23 cm) in length and have molted into their second natal down, which gives them a gray, woolly appearance. Tail and flight pin feathers are starting to appear and can show as much as one centimeter. The nestlings are able to walk on their tarso-metatarsus. When balancing they still use their wings. This is the stage when they begin to preen.

I returned on June 29 and saw two, two-and-a-half-week-old chicks about the size of a young chicken. At first I didn't notice the female, so I assumed she was out hunting. After setting up my camera, I began scanning the area and found the female perched on the limb of a live aspen twenty feet (6.10 m) south. She was so content that she never moved from her perch and at times even perched on one foot. I stayed for almost an hour.

Nineteen to twenty-two days after hatching, the birds are beginning to show dark contour feathers behind and below the eyes. The flight and tail feathers are emerging from the pin sheaths and stand out against the down feathers. By this time, the young can balance without using their wings. They spend time standing and preening. The nestlings will often flap their wings for three to five seconds, and they will peck at uneaten food.

A Northern Goshawk nestling twenty-four to twenty-six days after hatching.

Northern Goshawk nestlings, photographed June 25, 2014, at about a week-and-a-half old.

At twenty-four to twenty-six days, small dark feathers cover the auricular area. Yet the head and neck are still downy and a few dark feathers may show. The dark scapular feathers and wing coverts contrast with the light down feathers. The under-tail coverts begin showing, as do the feathers of the ventral tracts. The nestlings are about half the size of the adult birds at this stage. They stand at the nest edge and observe their surroundings. They also begin to stretch their legs and ball their feet into a fist. They may be able to feed themselves. At this stage, the adult female will roost away from the nest at night unless bad weather sets in.

Twenty-eight to thirty days after hatching, young Northern Goshawks still have downy feathers on the crown, but dark feathers appear around the nape of the neck. The coverts on the upper wings and back are feathered. Breast feathers are emerging from the ventral tracts, but the center of the breast and belly are still covered with down. The legs and both upper and under-tail coverts are still covered in down, but a few feathers are starting to appear. The nestlings spend more time preening and can scratch their heads with their talons. Young hawks pay attention to their parents exchanging food away from the nest. At this stage, the adult female will perch away from the nest but may become aggressive toward intruders.

The same young hawk with its mother, photographed June 25, 2014.

At thirty-two to thirty-four days, dark feathers emerge on the crown and around the corners of the mouth. The back and top of the wings are ninety percent feathered. All but the center of the breast is filled in with brown contour feathers. The under-tail coverts are present, as are feathers on the thighs. The tail is about two-thirds grown. The nestlings are capable of feeding themselves when the female is absent, often flapping their wings while hopping around the nest. At thirty-four or thirty-five days, the young begin moving along the branches near the nest, and at this stage they are called branchers.

The hawks' entire bodies are about ninety percent feathered at thirty-six to thirty-eight days, with some down feathers remaining on the sides of the neck, on the inner thighs, and in the under-wing covert areas. There may be a bit of down remaining just above the cere, but the rest of the head is feathered. The tail feathers are about three-quarters grown. The young hawks will be branching (walking on branches near the nest) and some males will be taking short flights. When the hawks are more than forty days post hatching they will look fully feathered, with down persisting in the under-wing coverts.

Two nestling Northern Goshawks, about twenty-five days old.

A nestling Northern Goshawk, twenty-eight days old.

The bird's bulging crop means it has recently eaten a good meal.

A nestling flapping its wings; this bird is approximately thirty days old.

This thirty-three-day-old nestling was photographed on July 12, 2011.

Fledging and Post-Fledging

When a young bird leaves its nest for the first time, it is considered a fledgling. Fledging behavior varies by type of bird. For example, young ducks, geese, grouse, and quail (all of which nest on the ground) hatch with eyes open, covered in down, and leave the nest within a few hours or days after hatching. The term for that is precocial, from the Latin *praecox*, meaning to ripen beforehand.

By comparison, birds that spend an extended period of time in their nest are termed altricial, from the Latin *altrix*, meaning nurse or wet nurse. Birds of this type often construct a nest off the ground; their nestlings are helpless at hatching, entirely dependent on their parents for warmth and protection. All hawks fit into this category (Terres, 1982).

The fledging period of young Northern Goshawks varies between thirty-four and forty-five days after hatching (Reynolds and Wight, 1978; Newton, 1979; and Brown and Amadon, 1968). At this time, the birds walk or hop to an adjacent branch, then take short flights between trees. Males often take their first

This single nestling was photographed on July 18, 2014. In this photo the bird is about thirty-six days old.

flights when they are thirty-six to forty days old, whereas females take the plunge a bit later, at thirty-nine to forty-two days after hatching (Reynolds and Wight, 1978). At fledging, the young hawks are shorter in length than their parents because their tails haven't fully grown.

In late July 1991, a pair of Northern Goshawks had constructed their nest in a large ponderosa pine on a private dude ranch south of Estes Park where I was working. I would periodically check the nest and watch the chicks' progress. I arrived at the nest the day they fledged. It was quite humorous to watch the young hawks take short flights and land awkwardly on branches. As soon as the adults flew off in search of food, a small flock of Gray Jays would fly in to harass the young hawks. One would fly in the front of a young hawk to get its attention, while a second jay would fly to the back and bite its tail. The hawks were clearly agitated, but there was nothing they could do about it.

Their chances of survival increase as they gain flight skills, enabling them to cover areas 328–984 feet (100–300 m) from the nest. Seven out of eight mortalities occur between three and ten days after fledging (Weins et al., 2006).

McClaren et al. (2005) found that fledglings on Vancouver Island completed their feather growth at seventy to seventy-five days post-fledging. Ninety-three percent of the radio-tagged young birds stayed within 656–984 feet (200–301 m) of their nests for the first three weeks after fledging and were often located either on the ground or in the lower canopy of the trees. Four weeks later, a little more than forty-two percent remained within that distance of their nest. Occasionally young birds would return to their nest trees. As their feathers hardened, they were often found higher in the canopy, and at times even perched in the treetops.

There was no indication that young hawks dispersed from their natal areas due to parental aggression. In other words, they left the area on their own accord. In 2001 and 2002, the young hawks left their nesting area eighty to ninety-six days post-fledging.

After fledging, the young hawks depend on their parents for food for thirty to forty days before leaving the nest area (Reynolds and Meslow, 1984).

As mentioned earlier, in 2011, I observed two nesting pairs of Northern Goshawks, both of which had two young. Unfortunately, one nest failed, but the other fledged one male and one female. Those two hawks were the young of the pair from the aforementioned Storm Pass Trail nest. When I saw the female leave the nest for the first time (fledge), it was quite anticlimactic. The young female simply walked onto the branches above the nest before taking a few short flights to nearby trees. I was hoping she would make a dramatic long-distance flight. When I arrived at the nest on July 14, the young male was still on its nest, and neither of the adult birds nor the recently fledged female were anywhere to be seen.

The next day, I arrived at the nest with Ryan Carpenter, a National Park Service employee, and Colorado State University Professor Alex Cruz, and found the nest empty. We searched the area for the second fledgling, yet found nothing. Just as we were about to leave, I heard a familiar cackle coming from a small Douglas fir thirty feet (9.14 m) from the nest. Knowing it was one of the young hawks, we set up our cameras and walked to the tree to find the little male had fledged and was now perched only six feet (1.83 m) above the ground. We took several photos and moved away.

I was fortunate to locate those two fledglings weekly for three weeks after they had fledged. During that time, they remained within 200 yards (182 m) of the nest. The last day that I saw the young hawks, the young female was perched on the ground with a red squirrel in her talons. I'm not sure if she caught the squirrel herself or if one of the adults brought it to her. After those young hawks fledged, the adult male Northern Goshawk seemed to spend time caring for the young female, whereas the adult female seemed to spend time caring for the young male.

I observed this thirty-nine-day-old hawk shortly after it left its nest for the first time.

The first fledgling from a nest in Rocky Mountain National Park in 2014.

It is always exciting to witness a young bird of prey make a kill. Young birds have to learn what size prey they are capable of overpowering. The success of the predator is often related to its ability to surprise its prey. When I've been fortunate to witness a predator attacking prey, more often than not, it is unsuccessful.

For example, on August 26, 2007, I was looking out my window and noticed a Wyoming ground squirrel near the deck. It seemed unusually wary, so I watched to see if the squirrel had been monitoring something in or near the yard. An instant later, the squirrel ran under my deck, and just then a juvenile Northern Goshawk flew past the window and landed in the neighbor's yard. The hawk waited a few moments, then flew out of sight.

In the spring of 2009, while on my way to work, a juvenile Northern Goshawk was attempting to catch pigeons near the eighteen-hole golf course in Estes Park. The area around the course is open, as you might expect. A retired falconer has a pigeon coop where the pigeons can be found year-round. However, pigeons are always on the lookout for potential predators. The hawk, in my opinion, made its approach from a little too far off, and the pigeons saw it coming. They exploded in all directions long before the hawk even came close. Instead of chasing the pigeons, the hawk alighted on the chicken coop roof, looking befuddled. It waited a few moments and then flew off.

During the fall and winter, young hawks need to figure out on their own how to catch prey off-guard. I've seen hawks perch in view of my feeders, searching for a bird to grasp. The hawks often use the sun to their advantage by perching with the sun behind them. The prey doesn't notice the hawk until it is captured.

The second fledgling from the Storm Pass Trail nest on July 10, 2009.

Fledgling raptors are quite the sight.

    After the nesting season, songbirds, on the other hand, often move in large flocks, enabling them to rely on each other for finding food and keeping a lookout for predators. Songbirds at a feeder, for example, are always on the lookout for potential danger. This is a great advantage when a hawk comes by to grab one of them for a quick meal. With all of the birds in one spot, at least a few are scouting for danger. Having lookouts may enable most, if not all, birds in the flock to evade an attack.

    For years, I've wondered why young accipiters are brown and white with barred under-wings and under-tail. After watching young hawks hunt in my yard during fall and winter, I understood. The coloring evolved as a camouflage in leafless trees for the rookie hunters. During fall and winter, their plumage perfectly matches their environment. After the hawks survive their first difficult winter, they molt into their colorful adult plumage that identifies them as adult birds. This may encourage mating, as birds know that an adult bird is more capable of finding the best territory to raise a family.

    In fall 2006, I watched a young Northern Goshawk land on the slightly angled, bare branch of an aspen. It instantly configured its body to parallel the angled branch. In the blink of an eye, the hawk flew down and caught a chipmunk. It appeared that the bird was attempting to blend into the branch.

If onlookers keep their distance, the birds will remain at ease.

Northern Goshawk habitat with a recently fledged hawk perched a few yards from its nest.

90

Two fledglings; the larger female is perched below its brother.

91

An adult Northern Goshawk with an Evening Grosbeak.

On September 6, 2009, when there were several Evening Grosbeaks on my deck feeders, a juvenile Northern Goshawk flew in and landed in the neighbor's aspen. Most of the finches flew away, but a few remained motionless. The hawk perched in the tree, surveying the yard. It must have seen one of the finches move, because the hawk singled out a bird on my deck and swooped in for the kill. As the hawk flew in, the finches remained still. Just before the capture, the single finch tried to fly away; the hawk swerved to the right, flaring its wings and tail to seemingly confuse the finch so that it didn't know which direction to escape. The finch was instantly caught, killed, plucked, and eaten on the deck.

Chapter Four

Northern Goshawks in Fall and Winter

Late fall and winter seem to be the best time see a Northern Goshawk, as the young birds, along with a few adults, disperse from their nesting areas and often fly near homes and into towns in search of something to eat. Northern Goshawks routinely move through areas such as Hawk Ridge in Duluth, Minnesota, and Hawk Mountain in east central Pennsylvania in the fall as they move south, searching for somewhere to spend the winter. According to the website HawkCount.org, most of the Northern Goshawk sightings at Hawk Ridge in Duluth from 2008–2011 occurred during October. However, at Hawk Mountain in Pennsylvania, the major sightings occurred in November. This difference in the migration timing is unclear. Throughout the northernmost portions of the Northern Goshawks' range, some move south in the fall. Yet, in the western and southern portions, some remain on their territories all year (Squires and Reynolds, 1997).

Squires and Ruggiero (1995) trapped five Northern Goshawks in the Medicine Bow National Forest in the Sierra Madre Mountains in south central Wyoming during their nesting season in 1992 and fitted them with transmitters. They defined migration as any bird that moved farther than 40.30 miles (65 km).

One female left her nesting area somewhere between August 26 and September 1, roughly fifty days after her young had fledged. She was seen on September 2 near Steamboat Springs, Colorado, 40.3 miles (65 km) south of her nest. She remained in that vicinity until October 27.

Before or after a snowstorm, the bird moved south and on November 4 was located approximately forty-three miles (70 km) away at an elevation of 9,997 feet (3,047 m). She continued to move south until she decided to spend the rest of the winter in an area between Rifle, Colorado, and Glenwood Springs, Colorado, at an elevation of between 8,495 and 9,708 feet (2,590–2,960 m). On March 23, the bird was spotted near the nest she had used in 1993.

A second female remained near her nest area until September 10, when she moved approximately 3.7 miles (six km) south. She remained there until October 2, when she was rediscovered 17.36 miles (28 km) south of her nest. On October 14, she was found 56.80 miles (140 km) from her nest in a forest of spruce, fir, and lodgepole pine. Before or after the snowstorm that prompted the previously mentioned birth to fly south, this bird moved as well and was not seen for the rest of the winter. However, on March 13, 1993, she was located near the Wyoming-Colorado border about 24.80 miles (40 km) south of her nesting area. On April 4, she was observed at her nest area.

In late August, a male was seen near his nest, yet by September 2 he had moved 10.54 miles (17 km) south. Two days later he had returned to his nest area. Two days after that, on September 6, he had moved 8.06 miles (13 km) south. Four days later, he had moved 13.40 miles (70 km) south into Colorado to an elevation of 10,876 feet (3,316 m). Then on April 12, 1993, he was seen roughly 6.20 miles (10 km) from the previous year's nest site. His transmitter failed and the bird was not seen again.

The results of that study suggest that Northern Goshawks nesting in south central Wyoming migrate in a southerly direction during the winter. This study also indicated that Northern Goshawks begin their migration in mid-September.

Underwood et al. (2006), studying Northern Goshawks in Utah, described their migration as any bird that moved sixty-two miles (100 km) or more without returning to its nesting area until the following nesting season. Semi-migrants moved as far as 100 miles (62 km), staying within a locale of 12.40–18.60 miles (20–30 km) for a few weeks before moving to another area, and returned to their nesting area the following season. The birds that left their nesting areas did so anywhere from August through December, with some moving 100 miles (62 km) within a few days.

Sedentary or year-round residents would expand their territories from roughly a square mile (2.58 km squared) to 3.1–15.5 miles (5–25 km). Underwood et al. (2006) tracked seven birds for more than a year and found that one made no migration the first year but did migrate the second year. Three migrated the first year and made the same migration the following year. The fifth bird stopped in an area it had used the previous year before finally choosing a wintering area 223.20 miles (360 km) farther south. Interestingly, seventy-five percent of wintering Northern Goshawks were found in either pinyon-juniper or maple and gamble oak habitat. The birds that stayed near their breeding territories year-round used habitat similar to the type they nested in.

Outside the nesting season, at times Northern Goshawks can be seen hunting species that they may not normally take during nesting season. These may include domestic poultry like chickens, peacocks, and other caged fowl, game birds like quail and pheasants not commonly found near Northern Goshawks nesting areas, and ducks and geese of various species that, again, are not commonly found near Northern Goshawk nests.

Rick Spowart, the Division of Parks and Wildlife officer in Drake, Colorado, told me that he routinely finds Northern Goshawks chasing his fowl on his property. In the fall of 1998 he found an adult Northern Goshawk attacking a peahen. "I heard a lot of squawking and looked out into the backyard to see a goshawk trying to kill a peahen," he said. "The peahen was at least twice the size of the hawk. Our Emden gander, who thought nothing of attacking people, went to the peahen's rescue and grabbed the hawk's wing with his bill and began beating the hawk with his own wings, while loudly squawking. The peahen was, of course, squawking along with the nearby chickens and the gander's mate who was encouraging him. It was too much for the hawk, who narrowly escaped after a good pummeling."

In the fall of 2000, a Northern Goshawk made another visit to his house and this time made a successful kill. "The goshawk had killed a large Barred Rock Rooster about 100 yards in front of my house. After the kill, the hawk began eating the head of the rooster. The rooster must have fled in a panic because it was killed in an area where the chickens never go. There was no way that the hawk could have carried that chicken to where it was being eaten because the chicken was too heavy for the hawk to have moved."

Another attack occurred in fall 2002 when an adult Northern Goshawk killed one of Rick's large roosters. "The goshawk killed a large Aracana Rooster near the front door of the house. The rooster was much larger than the hawk, which was busy eating the rooster's head when I came home. The hawk let me approach within ten feet before taking flight. As with the above mentioned chicken, chickens are seldom in the front yard because that is where the dogs live. The rooster must have desperately tried to escape the hawk by going near the dogs."

When grouse biologist Christian Hagen was living in Loveland, Colorado, he witnessed a Northern Goshawk attacking and trying to eat one of his chickens. Arriving home one afternoon, he found an adult Northern Goshawk plucking a still live chicken that the hawk had procured in Hagen's backyard. Because the chicken was so badly injured, Hagen let the hawk finish killing and eating its fill rather than trying to rescue the chicken.

A juvenile Northern Goshawk in late fall.

In June 2014, this adult male Northern Goshawk came into my yard searching for a meal of fledgling Black-billed Magpies. The adult magpies harassed him for several minutes until he flew off empty-handed.

    Another dramatic attack was witnessed by Gary C. Miller, former Research Leader and Statewide Ecologist for the Colorado Division of Wildlife (retired). "In the early 1980s I was researching Greater Prairie-Chickens in eastern Colorado to help recover what was then a state-endangered species. Early morning, I watched a lek, or 'booming ground,' that was along a low ridge. This lek was a couple hundred yards long. It was used daily by about twenty males. I was painstakingly trying to figure out the territory of the 'master cock.' I was trying to ascertain which one of them was most dominant and which would attract the most females. The master cock was one of about twenty birds on the lek. Finally, I was sure I had him located and placed my net in his territory, where I would be sure to capture the greatest number of females to radio-fit. The following morning, several colleagues joined me at about 3:00 a.m. We carefully approached the lek in separate vehicles from different vantage points and waited. At the first hint of light, we could hear the males booming. All was going according to plan. A bit more light, and I watched eight to ten female prairie-chickens ghosting through the sandsage, headed in the direction of the

After the nesting season ends, these large raptors can end up almost anywhere, including people's backyards.

Fledgling hawks can move several hundred miles from their nesting ground in search of productive areas to spend the winter.

master cock and our net. This promised to be our most successful netting to date! Then the somber voice of a colleague came on the radio: 'Wanna catch the goshawk?' I looked back to the lek. There, mantling over a now-dead master cock, was a Northern Goshawk, ripping apart the chicken. The females scattered—uncaptured and un-radioed. The other males, kept right on booming. My colleagues and I watched the show until the goshawk ate its fill and flew off, and were left to wonder, shades of Rick in *Casablanca*: of all the males on all the leks in all of Yuma County, he shows up at this one. And—what in the heck was a Northern Goshawk doing in the middle of the prairie?"

Rehabilitation

On the afternoon of October 4, 2004, while birding in RMNP with friends from Texas, my pager went off. I recognized the number as that of the Sweet Memorial Building at the YMCA of the Rockies. Gail Albers, the YMCA program director, told me that some children were eating lunch on a picnic table when a large hawk landed in the middle of their table. The kids were startled and stepped away just as the hawk took off and landed on a nearby roof.

As I arrived at the Sweet Memorial Building, the employees directed me to the rooftop, where the hawk was perched. In the meantime, Gail had found a large box that I could put the hawk into if I caught him. As soon as I saw the bird, I identified it as an adult Northern Goshawk. I climbed up on some logs at the side of the building, hoping to get onto the roof to grasp the hawk. At one point the hawk and I were about two feet (0.61 m) apart looking at each other.

I began talking to the hawk, explaining that I was there to help and wasn't going to hurt him. He apparently didn't believe me, as he awkwardly flew a few yards to a ponderosa pine and landed on a branch just out of my reach. I threw a stick up at him, hoping he would fly again, but he just sat there. A YMCA employee climbed the tree and scared the bird into flying several yards toward a nearby lodge.

I ran like a deer, hurtling over small bushes, trying to keep up with the bird. Just before I caught up to him, he flew into the side of the lodge and fell to the ground. I reached down and picked him up and quickly palpated his wing bones to ensure nothing was broken. Next I checked his fat level to see how healthy he was. He was quite thin, seemingly only skin, bones, and feathers. When a bird is fat and healthy, the breast will feel like that of a store-bought chicken, fat and rounded. Conversely, when a bird is thin, the keel (breastbone) will be sharp. This hawk was so thin he appeared to have no muscle at all on his breast.

I slowly placed him in the box, and my friends and I returned to my house. I put together one of my large pet carriers, placed a large, thick towel on the bottom, and added a large water dish. I slowly opened the box and saw the hawk lying with its head on the bottom of the box, eyes closed. My first thought was that the poor bird had died.

A Northern Goshawk with West Nile Virus, prior to being captured. Photo ©Joe Halt

I asked Anne, one of my birder friends who was with me at the time, to fill a syringe with water that I would use to give the bird a drink. I put my hands around the bird's wings and gently lifted him from the box. The bird squirmed a bit and then stopped and looked up at me. Using the syringe, I gave him some water. This is done by opening the bird's mouth and placing the end of the syringe behind its tongue, which prevents any water from going into the bird's air hole.

Birds have an air hole at the base of the tongue that allows them to breath when their mouth is open. After giving the bird water, I laid him on the towel so he was facing the door of the pet carrier. I then rolled up a second towel and formed a "U" shape around

Scott hand-feeding an adult hawk with West Nile Virus. *Photo ©Susan Rashid*

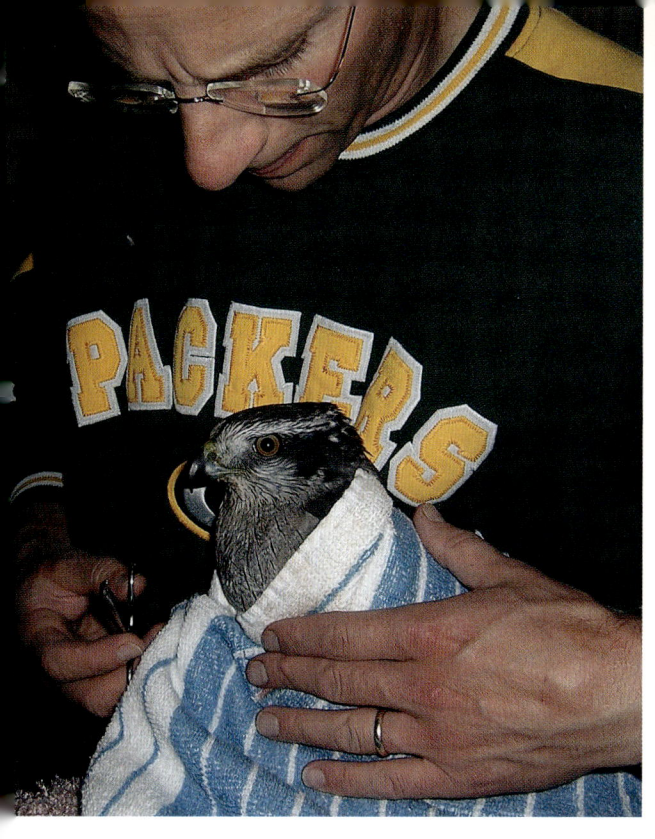

This bird had to be fed twice a day for six weeks before it could even stand. *Photo ©Susan Rashid*

him, making sure the bottom of the "U" was under his chin. That way the bird could rest lying flat and facing the front of the pet carrier so I could assist him when needed. I also placed a second towel under the tip of the bird's tail so that he could expel his feces without clogging his vent.

Finding no injuries, my initial thought was that he might have West Nile Virus. The Birds of Prey Foundation in Broomfield, Colorado, had recently admitted several birds with West Nile Virus. I called the founder and president, Sigrid Ueblacker, and described the bird's symptoms. She said that it sounded like West Nile Virus. She also explained that the foundation was experimenting with a blood pressure medication for the birds and offered to share her supply.

The theory at that time was that if we could increase the bird's blood pressure, it might also increase the bird's appetite, enabling it to begin eating on its own. I placed the medication in a small amount of meat and fed it to the hawk. The poor bird was in such rough shape that it could not even stand up. Every day I got up 4:30 a.m. before work to prepare the bird's breakfast and feed him. His breakfast and dinner were the same—quail. I would first cut up a quail into small pieces, add the medication, and then hand-feed the hawk. This was a slow and arduous task that took an hour every morning and afternoon.

To feed the hawk, I would place him on the counter, cradled under my armpit. With the index finger of my left hand I would lift his upper mandible and place a small amount of watered quail on the back of his tongue so that his gag reflex made him swallow. I repeated this every morning and afternoon for three weeks before the poor bird could even stand up. Several times when I looked in on him, I thought he had expired. Then, as I opened the carrier door, he would look up at me. This happened almost daily during the first few days.

After the first week, he began lying with his eyes open, and later he began to stand a few minutes each day. The most exciting day was October 25, when the hawk was able to stand on his own and aware of his surroundings. I took him to the Birds of Prey Foundation, where he was placed in a large flight cage for about six months, enabling him to exercise and gain enough strength to be returned to the area he came from. After the rehabilitation period, I picked up the hawk from the Foundation and released him on the edge of the YMCA grounds bordering Rocky Mountain National Park. I was so impressed that this bird had recovered and could be released back into the wild.

A few years earlier, in the fall of 2001, Sigrid had called to tell me that two Northern Goshawks—a young male and female—were ready for release. The area around RMNP has several good places to release Northern Goshawks back into the wild. I normally choose the MacGregor Ranch, a historic cattle ranch on the north side of Estes Park adjacent to the national park and Roosevelt National Forest. Birds of prey typically seen on that ranch include Golden Eagles, Red-tailed Hawks, Peregrine Falcons, Prairie Falcons, Great Horned Owls, Northern Pygmy Owls, Saw-whet Owls, and of course Northern Goshawks. The property is far from houses and cars that the birds often crash into.

Later that morning, I arrived at the foundation and went to the area they call the loafing shed, a series of connected rooms where injured accipiters are housed. This works well for these types of birds because it is dark and quiet. (Accipiters are often high strung and react to every little movement around them. If you are trying to heal an injured accipiter, it needs to be in an area away from people.) Sigrid captured the male Northern Goshawk, and I placed a Fish and Wildlife Service aluminum band on the bird's leg. He was taken out of his cage and placed in a pet carrier to be transported to the ranch for release. She returned to the loafing shed to capture the female hawk, which she did with ease. She brought the bird out to me, and I banded her, too. Then it got interesting. I knew that Northern Goshawks were quick, but until that morning I had no idea how quick. Sigrid was holding the bird with both hands as I opened the pet carrier. She placed the hawk into the pet carrier head first, as far back as she could reach. Before she could close the door, the hawk turned around and flew out. Within a second or two it had flown a few yards and landed on top of one of the adjacent cages. The bird sat for a few minutes and looked around before flying off.

The following day, Sigrid received a call from a farmer who had caught the hawk inside his chicken coop. Noticing the leg band, he called the foundation and returned the hawk to Sigrid. He said that he didn't want to mess up a research project. The hawk was kept over the winter and re-released the following spring. Talk about a second chance at freedom!

On May 9, 2011, I received a call from Estes Park residents David and Nancy Bargen, who told me that a large owl in their yard was unable to fly. I happened to be a few miles from their house, so I made my way there. I grabbed my net as David pointed to a large bird hiding under a large Blue Spruce. Since the bird was in a fenced yard, I assumed it had crashed into a window while chasing a bird. As I approached the bird, it ran from under the tree and tried to climb a chain-link fence. Identifying it as a juvenile Northern Goshawk, I ran over and placed the net over it. With one hand under the net, I grasped the bird's legs. Once its legs were secured, I picked him up and took off the net.

The bird was unable to stand without using one of its wings to balance itself. Not having a pet carrier in my truck, I called friend and fellow birder Gary Mathews and asked him to drive me to my house as I held the bird. While waiting for Gary, I palpated the bird's wings to make sure that nothing was broken, and then I showed David and Nancy a few anatomical details about how to identify a Northern Goshawk. Then I placed a towel over the hawk's head to help keep it calm. Birds tend to calm down when they can't see anything that could cause them stress.

After we arrived at the house, I had Gary set up a large pet carrier with towels and a water dish. I noticed that the hawk was quite unstable, but knowing what stress can do, I decided to let him rest while I retrieved my car.

A juvenile Northern Goshawk perched in a flight cage at the Birds of Prey Foundation.

The hawk had likely experienced severe head trauma. Since it was unstable, I began to hand-feed him twice a day. I cut rats and quail into small pieces and, using forceps, fed the hawk for the next six days until he could stand well enough to feed himself. On June 2, 2011, the bird was transferred to a larger exercise cage at the Birds of Prey Foundation. Unfortunately, that hawk never recovered well enough to be released and had to be euthanized. When rehabilitating birds, the one thing that always needs to be kept in mind is the bird's quality of life. Not all birds do well in captivity, and euthanasia may be the best thing.

On August 31, 2012, I received a call from one of the employees of the Estes Park Library who told me of a large hawk that had just hit one of the windows and was standing on the sidewalk outside a window. It was, in fact, a young male Northern Goshawk. I walked up to the bird and began talking to it, explaining that I was there to help. The bird was looking at me in a way that made me think he was actually listening. I then slowly reached down and covered it with a towel. The bird tried to walk away, but I put my hands around him and picked him up.

I palpated his wings to make sure nothing was broken and placed him in my pet carrier. Meanwhile, my wife, Susan, got a large carrier ready at home. She placed a few dark towels on the bottom, along with a water dish. A perch is sometimes used, depending on the injury. If the bird is able to eat on his own, a rat or quail is placed in the carrier with the bird. If not, the food is cut up into small pieces so the bird doesn't have to do any work to eat.

As the bird becomes stronger, it can be fed whole prey—rats or rabbits from a pet store or another rehabilitator. Quail is also an option, but I have learned over the years that when you feed accipiters quail, they want it for every meal. Northern Goshawks are primarily bird eaters and love quail because they don't often get it in the wild. A rat or rabbit will keep the birds full longer than a quail.

Before releasing any young bird of prey back to the wild, I make sure it can identify and kill its prey. To do this, I simply place live prey in the cage, and it doesn't take long before the bird's instincts take over. This hawk was in my care for only three weeks before I released him in my backyard. I had seen several hawks migrating through the area, so it was as good a place as any. But first I banded him, as I do with every rehabilitated bird.

Occasionally, I have a bird that won't eat on its own, like the Sharp-shinned Hawk I nursed back to health several years ago. In that case, after I placed it in the flight cage, I added a live House Sparrow. The hawk instantly caught and ate the songbird. After that, it ate everything I placed in the cage, alive or dead. Sometimes you just have to be smarter than the bird you are helping.

A juvenile hawk in a pet carrier resting, after it had crashed into a window.

Mortality and Longevity

Northern Goshawks are sometimes found dead. Causes of death include being shot, starvation, disease, trauma, trapping, collisions, and being poisoned.. It's interesting that nobleman or yeoman treasured Northern Goshawks for falconry. However, when guns were invented, all birds of prey were considered man's competitors and were often shot and killed. In 1913, the Migratory Bird Treaty Act was passed, which protected hawks from hunting. Yet the killing continued in large numbers until the fall of 1934, according to a 1963 issue of *Boy's Life* magazine. On a single afternoon in mid-November 1926, sixty-seven Northern Goshawks were killed at Blue Mountain near Drehersville, Schuylkill County, Pennsylvania. The following year on October 19, 1927, four hawks were killed, and three days later sixteen more were killed at the same location (Sutton, 1931). In the early 1930s, the Pennsylvania State Game Commission placed a bounty on Northern Goshawks, allowing them to be shot at will. Between November 1, 1936, and April 1, 1937, over 280 Northern Goshawks had been shot and killed.

Meng (1959) claimed that Northern Goshawks and other accipiters are "exceedingly wary, and are seldom seen even in areas where they are abundant," and therefore rarely shot. He found that the majority of hawks were caught in pole traps. Pole traps are secured to a fence post, often near a game farm. When a hawk lands on this perch, the trap closes around the bird's leg, often breaking it. The bird can't fly away, and it hangs by its broken leg until it dies or is eaten by an animal. Most of these hawks were young birds attracted to poultry farms in hopes of an easy meal.

Northern Goshawks are occasionally found dead from starvation. Weins et al. (2006) found three fledgling Northern Goshawks that had died of starvation and two more that had died from unknown sources of physical trauma. In 2009, Colorado Department of Parks and Wildlife officer Rick Spowart of Drake, Colorado, found a juvenile Northern Goshawk dead, apparently of starvation, near one of his pheasant coops.

The same hawk, in the flight cage, prior to its release.

On December 24, 1992, Squires and Ruggiero (1995) recovered the carcass of a Northern Goshawk that had died from blunt force trauma. The bird had acute hemorrhaging under its right wing. The bird's ribs on both sides were broken, with one puncturing its lung. It also had a broken neck. The guess was that this trauma was caused by another raptor, possibly an eagle or large falcon such as a gyr or peregrine.

At times, hawks and owls will fight to the death. Rev. C. W. G. Eifrig (1907) in Bent (1937) tells of a battle between a Barred Owl and a Goshawk: "One morning last February, Mr. Hugo Paeseler, a farmer, ongoing out into the woods adjoining his farm, noticed a space of about ten to fifteen feet square, where the snow had recently been much disturbed, deeply plowed up from some great commotion. That a fierce fight had been going on but a short while before was evident from the liberal quantities of blood sprinkled on the snow and the masses of feathers, single and in whole bunches, lying about and adhering to bushes and trees. On looking around for the principals of the fight, he found about ten feet away in one direction a goshawk, lying on the snow with wings extended and frozen stiff. About ten feet away from the scene of hostilities, in the opposite direction, he found an owl, more damaged than the hawk, but still warm. It had alighted after the fight on a small spruce and fallen off, as the snow showed, and with its last strength crawled into a small log, lying with its hallow part conveniently near."

On the afternoon of August 26, 2002, I received a call from Jim Thompson, a retired superintendent of Rocky Mountain National Park, who told me that a friend of his had found a large hawk lying dead under a telephone pole. About a half hour later, Jim and I arrived on the scene and found a dead juvenile female Northern Goshawk. On the pole were two transformers. What often happens is that as a bird takes off from the pole, a wing and tail or both wings touch the two wires and the bird is electrocuted, which is what appeared to have happened. Fortunately, Estes Park has since retrofitted the telephone poles to eliminate this hazard.

Other Northern Goshawks have been fatally infected with West Nile Virus as it spread from eastern North America through the West. And sometimes young hawks are found dead under their nests, cause unknown (Reynolds and Wight 1978).

Predation by Animals and Other Birds

There are several accounts of Northern Goshawks being killed by both birds and animals. Weins et al. (2006) recovered three juvenile Northern Goshawks that had been killed by Great Horned Owls. Boals et al. (2005) found two adult Northern Goshawks killed by Great Horned Owls. In 2011, I observed a Northern Goshawk nest that failed. There was nothing to make me think that an animal had climbed the tree, so I presumed the young hawks were taken by a Great Horned Owl.

Erdman et al. (1998) found that virtually all of the reproductive failures in their study in northeastern Wisconsin were due to fisher predation. Fishers are large and aggressive members of the weasel family. The study cited four female Northern Goshawks killed at their nests by fishers. Another reason for the loss of nestling Northern Goshawks was falconer abductions, with seventeen percent of nestlings taken in 1979. Like Boals and Weins, Erdman also found that Great Horned Owls had killed adult, nestling, and fledgling Northern Goshawks.

Boals et al. (2006) found that the pine martin (a member of the weasel family, larger than a long-tailed weasel but smaller than a fisher) and inclement weather in Minnesota were causes of mortality. McClaren (2004) noted that a Northern Goshawk nest on Queen Charlotte Island was ravaged by a raccoon.

On a more upbeat note, according to the Bird Banding Laboratory in Laurel, Maryland, the oldest wild Northern Goshawk on record as of 2010 was sixteen years and five months. The bird was banded in New York on May 29, 1973, and found dead on October 29, 1999. The second oldest was sixteen years and four months. That bird was banded in New Jersey on October 20, 1974, and recovered in Pennsylvania on October 29, 1990.

I have studied the Northern Goshawk for over twenty years. Ever since seeing my first wild Northern Goshawk, I have been impressed by their beauty, strength, speed, and agility. My hope is that after picking up this book, readers will feel the same way.

Animals such as pine martins feed on nestling and adult Northern Goshawks. *Photo by Wayne Johnson.*

Scientific Names of Birds, Plants, and Animals

Birds
American Crow (*Corvus brachyrhynchos*)
American Kestrel (*Falco sparverius*)
American Robin (*Turdus migratorius*)
American Woodcock (*Scolopac minor*)
Araucana Rooster (*Gallus inauris*)
Band-tailed Pigeon (*Columba fasciata*)
Barred Owl (*Strix varia*)
Barred Rock Chicken (*Gallus domesticus*)
Black-billed Magpie (*Pica pica*)
Black Duck (*Anas rubripes*)
Blue-winged Teal (*Anas discors*)
Black Tern (*Chlidonias niger*)
Bonaparte's Gull (*Larus philadelphia*)
Boreal Owl (*Aegolius funereus*)
Broad-winged Hawk (*Buteo platypterus*)
Broad-tailed Hummingbird (*Selasphorus platycercus*)
Burrowing Owl (*Athene cunicularia*)
California Gull (*Larus californicus*)
California Quail (*Callipepla californica*)
Cassin's Finch (*Carpodacus cassinii*)
Cave Swallow (*Petrochelidon fulva*)
Chipping Sparrow (*Spizella passerina*)
Common Eider (*Somateria mollissima*)
Common Goldeneye (*Bucephala clangula*)
Common Grackle (*Quiscalus quiscula*)
Common Nighthawk (*Chordeiles minor*)
Common Poorwill (*Phalaenoptilus nuttallii*)
Common Raven (*Corvus corax*)
Common Yellowthroat (*Geothlypis trichas*)
Cooper's Hawk (*Accipiter cooperii*)
Coot (*Fulica americana*)
Dark-eyed Juncos (*Junco hyemalis*)
Downy Woodpeckers (*Picoides pubescens*)
Dusky Grouse (*Dendragapus obscurus*)
Eastern Meadowlark (*Sturnella magma*)
Eastern Screech Owl (*Otus asio*)
Eurasian Collared Dove (*Streptopelia decaocto*)
European Starling (*Sturnus vulgaris*)
Flammulated Owl (*Otus flammeolus*)
Forester's Tern (*Sterna forsteri*)

Golden-crowned Kinglet (*Regulus satrapa*)
Gray Jay (*Perisoreus canadensis*)
Gray Partridge (*Perdix perdix*)
Great Gray Owl (*Strix nebulosa*)
Great Horned Owl (*Bubo virginiianus*)
Greater Yellowlegs (*Tringa melanoleuca*)
Greater Green Heron (*Butorides virescens*)
Green-tailed Towhees (*Pipilo chlorurus*)
Hairy Woodpecker (*Picoides villosus*)
Harris's Hawk (*Parabuteo unicinctus*)
Harris's Sparrow (*Zonotrichia querula*)
Hermit Thrush (*Catharus guttatus*)
Herring Gull (*Larus argentatus*)
Horned Lark (*Eremophila alpestris*)
House Sparrow (*Passer domesticus*)
House Wren (*Troglodytes aedon*)
Killdeer (*Charadrius vociferus*)
King Rail (*Rallus elegans*)
Leach's Storm-Petrel (*Oceanodroma leucorhoa*)
Lesser Goldfinch (*Carduelis psaltria*)
Lesser Yellowlegs (*Tringa flavipes*)
Long-eared Owl (*Asio otus*)
MacGillivary's Warbler (*Oporonis tolmiei*)
Malay Fish Owl (*Bubo ketupu*)
Marbled Murrlet (*Brachyramphus marmoratus*)
Mountain Bluebirds (*Sialia currucoides*)
Mountain Chickadee (*Poecile gambeli*)
Mountain Quail (*Oreortyx pictus*)
Mourning Dove (*Zenaida macroura*)
Northern Cardinal (*Cardinalis cardinalis*)
Northern Flicker (*Colaptes auratus*)
Northern Goshawk (*Accipiter gentilis*)
Northern Mockingbird (*Mimus polyglottos*)
Northern Harrier (*Circus cyaneus*)
Northern Pintail (*Anas acuta*)
Northern Saw-whet Owl (*Aegolius acadicus*)
Northern Shrike (*Lanius excubitor*)
Northwest Crow (*Corvus cairinus*)
Ovenbird (*Seiurus aurocapillus*)
Passenger Pigeon (*Ectopistes migratorius*)
Peregrine Falcon (*Falco peregrinus*)
Pileated Woodpecker (*Dryocopus pileatus*)
Pine Grosbeak (*Pinicola enucleator*)
Pine Siskin (*Carduelis pinus*)
Purple Gallinule (*Porphyrula martinica*)
Purple Martin (*Progne subis*)
Pygmy Nuthatch (*Sitta pygmaea*)
Red-breasted Nuthatch (*Sitta Canadensis*)
Red Crossbill (*Loxia curvitostra*)
Red-napped Sapsucker (*Sphyrapicus nuchalis*)
Red Shouldered Hawk (*Buteo lineatus*)
Red-tailed Hawk (*Buteo jamaicensis*)

Red-winged Blackbirds (*Agelaius phoeniceus*)
Ring-necked Pheasant (*Phasianus colchicus*)
Rock Pigeon (*Columbis livia*)
Rock ptarmigan (*Lagopus mutus*)
Rosy finch (*Leucosticte* sp.)
Rusty Blackbird (*Euphagus carolinus*)
Ruby-crowned Kinglet (*Regulus calendula*)
Ruffed Grouse (*Bonasa umbellus*)
Sharp-shinned Hawk (*Accipiter striatus*)
Short-eared Owl (*Asio flammeus*)
Spotted Owl (*Strix occidentalis*)
Spotted Sandpiper (*Actitis macularia*)
Spruce Grouse (*Falcipennis canadensis*)
Stellar's Jay (*Cyanocitta Stelleri*)
Swainson's Thrush (*Catharus ustulatus*)
Swainson's Hawk (*Buteo swainsoni*)
Swamp Sparrow (*Melospiza Georgiana*)
Three-toed Woodpecker (*Picoides tridactylus*)
Townsend's Solitaire (*Myadestes townsendi*)
Varied Thrush (*Lxoreus naevius*)
Veery (*Catharus fuscescens*)
Virginia Rail (*Rallus limicola*)
Western Tananger (*Piranga ludoviciana*)
Whip-poor-will (*Caprimulgus vociferous*)
White-breasted Nuthatch (*Sitta americana*)
White-crowned Sparrow (*Zonotrichia leucophrys*)
White-faced Ibis (*Plegadis chihi*)
White-tailed Ptarmigan (*Lagopus leucurus*)
Williamson's Sapsucker (*Sphyrapicus thyroideus*)
Willow Ptarmagan (*Lagopus lagopus*)
Wilson's Snipe (*Gallinago delecta*)
Yellow-rumped Warblers (*Dendroica coronata*)

Trees and Shrubs

American Beech (*Fagus grandifolia*)
Balsam Poplar (*Populus balsamifera*)
Black Birch (*Betula lenta*)
Black Spruce (*Picea mariana*)
California Black Oak (*Quercus kelloggii*)
Common Juniper (*Juniperus communis*)
Cottonwood trees (*Populus* sp.)
Douglas Fir (*Pseudotsuga menziesii*)
Engelmann Spruce (*Picea engelmanni*)
European Larch (*Larix decidua*)
Gamblles Oak (*Quercus gambelii*)
Juniper Tree (*Juniperus scopulorum*)
Lodgepole Pine (*Pinus contorta latifolia*)
Mountain Alder (*Alnus tenuifolia*)
Oak (*Quercus* sp.)
Paper Birch (*Betula papyrifera*)
Ponderosa Pine (*Pinus ponderosa*)

Poplar (*Populaus* sp.)
Quaking Aspen (*Populus tremuloides*)
River Birch (*Betula nigra*)
Russian Olive (*Elaeagnus angustifolia*)
Sub Alpine fir (*Abies lasiocarpa*)
Sycamore tree (*Platanus wrightii*))
Wax Currant (*Ribes cereum*)
White Cedar (*Thuja occidentalis*)
White Spruce (*Picea glauca*)

Animals
Bobcats (*Lynx rufus*)
Deer Mouse (*Peromyscus maniculatus*)
Douglas Squirrel (*Tamiasciurus douglasii*
Eastern Chipmunk (*Tamias striatus*)
Elk (*Cervus elaphus*)
Flying Squirrel (*Scuiriopterus scuriopterus*)
Fisher (*Martes pennanti*)
Golden Mantled Ground Squirrel (*Spermophilus lateralis*)
Gray Jay (*Perisoreus canadensis*)
Hispid Cotton Rat (*Sigmodon hispidus*)
House Mouse (*Mus musculus*)
Harvest Mouse (*Reithrodontomys* sp.)
Least Chipmunk (*Eutamias minimus*)
Long-tailed Vole (*Microtus longicaudus*)
Mountain Lion (*Felis concolor*)
Meadow Vole (*Microtus pennsylvanicus*)
Montane Vole (*Microtus montanus*).
Northern Bog Lemming (*Synaptomys borealis*)
Northern Flying Squirrel (*Glycomys sabrinus*)
Northern Pocket Gopher (*Thomomys talpoides*)
Northern Pygmy Mouse (*Baiomys taylori*)
Pine Martin (*Martes americana*)
Pack Rat (*Neotoma cinerea*)
Red Squirrel (*Tamiasciurus hudsonicus*)
Raccoon (*Procyon lotor*)
Red-backed Vole (*Clethrionomys gapperi*),
Smoky Shrew (*Sorex fumeus*)
Snowshoe Hare (*Lepus americanus*)
Short-tailed Shrew (*Blarina brevicauda*)
Southern Red-backed Vole (*Myodes gapperi*)
Shrews (*Sorax* sp.)
Texas Kangaroo Rat (*Dipodomys* sp.)
Western Jumping Mouse (*Zapus princeps*)
Weasel (*Mustela* sp.)
White-footed Mouse (*Peromyscus leucopus*)
Woodland Mouse (*Peromyscus leucopus*)
Wyoming Ground Squirrel (*Urocitellus elegans*)

References

Aigner, P. A., M. L. Morrison, L. S. Hall, and W. M. Block. "Great Horned Owl Food Habits at Mono Lake, California." *The Southwestern Naturalist* 39 (3) (1994): 286–288.

Baker, J. K. "The Manner and Efficiency of Raptors Depredations on Bats." *The Condor* (1962): 500–504.

Beier, P., J. E. Drennan. "Forest Structure and Prey in Foraging Areas of Northern Goshawks." *Ecological Applications* 7 (2) (1997): 564–571.

Bent, A. C. *Life History of North American Birds of Prey* (Part One). New York: Dover Publications, 1938.

Bent, A. C. *Life History of North American Birds of Prey* (Part Two) New York: Dover Publications, 1938.

Bloom, P. H., and S. J. Hawks. "Food habits of Nesting Golden Eagles in Northwest California and Northwestern Nevada." *Journal of Raptor Research* 16 (4) (1982): 110-115.

Boal, C. W. "A Photographic and Behavioral Guide to Aging Nestling Northern Goshawk." *Studies in Avian Biology* 16 (1994): 32–40.

Boal, C. W., D. E. Anderson, P. L. Kennedy and A. M. Roberson. "Northern Goshawk Ecology in the Western Great Lakes Region." *Studies in Avian Biology* 31 (2006): 126–134.

Boal, C. W., D. E. Andersen and P. L. Kennedy. "Productivity and Mortality of Northern Goshawks in Minnesota." *Journal of Raptor Research* 39 (2) (2005): 222–228.

Brown, L., and D. Amadon. "Eagle, Hawks and Falcons of the World." London: *Country Life Books*, 1968.

Cade, T. J. "Ecology of the Peregrine and Gyrfalcon Populations in Alaska." *Zool* (1960) 63: 151–290.

Cameron, F. S. "Birds of Custer and Dawson Counties, Montana." *Auk* 24 (1907): 260–269.

Craighead, J. J., and F. C. Craighead Jr. *Hawks, Owls and Wildlife*. Mineola, NY: Dover Books, 1969.

Dixon, J. B. and R. E. Dixon. "Nesting of the Western Goshawk in California." *The Condor* XL, Jan.–Feb. (1938): 3–11.

Eakle. W. L. and T. G. Grubb. "Prey Remains from Golden Eagle Nests in Central Arizona." *Western Birds* 17 (2) (1986): 87–89, 1986.

Eng, R. L. and G. Gullion. "The Predation of Goshawks Upon Ruffed Grouse on the Cloquet Forest Research Center, Minnesota." *Wilson Bull* 74 (3) (1962): 227–242.

Erdman et al. "Productivity, Population Trend, and Status of Northern Goshawks, Accipiter Gentiles, in Northeastern Wisconsin." *The Canadian Field Naturalist* (1998): 17–27.

Errington, P. L. "Food Habits of Southern Wisconsin Raptors." Part One. Owls. *The Condor* (1932): 176–186.

Ethier, T. J. "Breeding Ecology and Habitat of Northern Goshawks (*Accipiter gentilis laingi*) on Vancouver Island: A Hierarchical Approach." M.Sc. thesis (1999), University of Victoria.

Graham, R. T. et al. "The Northern Goshawk in Utah: Habitat Assessment and Management Recommendations." USDA Forest Service (1999): 1–42.

Golet, G. H., H. T. Golet, and A. M. Colton. "Immature Northern Goshawk Captures, Kills and Feed on Adult-sized Wild Turkey." *Journal of Raptor Research* 37 (4) (2003): 337–340.

Gromme, O. J. "The Goshawk (*Astur Atricaillus Atricaillus*) Nesting in Wisconsin." *Auk* 52 (1935): 15–20.

Hargis, C. D., C. McCarthy, and R. D. Perloff. "Home Ranges of Habitats of Northern Goshawks in Eastern California." *Studies of Avian Biology* 6 (1994): 66–74.

Iverson, G. C., G. D. Hayward, K, Titus, E. Degayner, R. E. Lowell, D. Coleman Crocker-Bedford, P. F. Schempf, and J, Lindell. "Conservation Assessment for the Northern Goshawk in Southeastern Alaska." (1996) USDA.

James A. Thrailkill, Lawrence S. Andrews, and Rita M. Claremont. "Diet of Breeding Northern Goshawks in the Coast Range of Oregon." *Journal of Raptor Research* 34 (4) (2000): 339–340.

Jehl, J. R. Jr. and B. G. Murray Jr. "Response: Evolution of Sexual Size Dimorphism." *Auk* 106 (1989): 155–157.

Johnsgard, P. A. *North American Owls*. Second Edition. Washington DC: Smithsonian Institute Press, 2002.

Kennedy, P. L. "Northern Goshawk (*Accipiter gentilis*). A Technical Conservation Assessment." Dept. of Fishery and Wildlife Biology (2003): 1–146. University of Fort Collins.

Latham, R. "The Food of Predaceous Animals in Northeastern United States." Pennsylvania Game Commission, Final Report, P-R Proj. 36-R Rept. (1950): 1–69.

Lewis, S. B. "Delivery and Consumption of a Pigeon Guillemot by Nesting Northern Goshawks in Southeastern Alaska." *Wilson Bull*. 115 (4) (2003): 483–485.

Lewis, S. B., K. Titus, M. K. Fuller. "Northern Goshawk Diet during the Nesting Season in Southeastern Alaska." *Journal of Wildlife Management* 70 (4) (2006): 1151–1160.

McClaren, E. L., P. L. Kennedy, D. D. Dolye. "Northern Goshawk (*Accipiter Gentilis Laingi*) Post-Fledging Areas on Vancouver Island, British Columbia." *Journal of Raptor Research* 39 (3) (2005): 253–263.

McGowan, J. D. "Distribution, Density and Productivity of Goshawks in Interior Alaska." Alaska Dept. of Fish and Game, P-R Proj. Rep. (1975): W-17-445.

Meng, H. K. "Food Habits of Nesting Cooper's Hawks and Goshawks in New York and Pennsylvania." *Wilson Bull* 71 (2) (1959): 169–174.

Meng, H. K. "The Cooper's Hawk Accipiter Cooperii (Bonaparte)" Unpublished PhD thesis (1951), Cornell University: 202.

Newton, I. "Population Ecology of Raptors." Vermillion, SD: Buteo Books, 1979.

Palmer, R. S., *Handbook of North American Birds*. Vol. 4. "Diurnal Raptors" Part 1. New Haven, CT: Yale University Press, 1988.

Penteriani, V. "The Annual and Diel Cycles of Goshawk Vocalizations at Nest Sites." *Journal of Raptor Research* 35 (1) (2001): 24–30.

Pyle, P. *Identification Guide to North American Birds*. Part 1. Slate Creek Press, 1997.

Reynolds, R. T. and E. C. Meslow. "Partitioning of Food and Niche Characteristics of Coexisting Accipiter During Breeding." *Auk* 101 (1984): 761–799.

Reynolds, R. T., R. T. Graham, M. H. Reiser, R. L. Bassett, P. L. Kennedy, D. A. Boyce, G. Goodwin, R. Smith, and E. L. Fisher. "Management Recommendations for the Northern Goshawk in the Southern United States." 1-90. USDA Forest Service Gen. Tech. rep. RM–217 (1992). Rocky Mountain Forest and Range Experiment Station, Fort Collins, CO.

Reynolds, R.T. J. D. Weins, S. M. Joy, S. R. Salafsky. "Sampling Considerations for Demographics and Habitat Studies of Northern Goshawks." *Journal of Raptor Research* 39 (3) (2005): 274–285.

Reynolds, R. T. and H. M. Wight. "Distribution, Density, and Productivity of Accipiter Hawks Breeding in Oregon." *Wilson Bull* 90 (2) (1978), 182–196.

Reynolds, R. T. "Sexual Dimorphism in Accipiter hawks: A New Hypothesis." *The Condor* 74 (1972): 191–197.

Rohner, C. and F. I. Doyle, "Food Stressed Great Horned Owl Kills Adult Goshawk: Exceptional

Observation or Community Process?" Journal of Raptor Research 26 (4) (1992): 261–263.

Rohner, C. and F. I. Doyle, "Method of Locating Great Horned Owl Nests in the Boreal Forest." *Journal of Raptor Research* 26 (1) (1992): 33–35.

Rosenfield, R. N., J. Boelefeldt, D. R. Trexel, and T. C. J. Doolittle. "Breeding Distribution and Nest-site Habitat of Northern Goshawks in Wisconsin." *Journal of Raptor Research* 32 (3) (1998): 189–194.

Salafsky, S. R., R. T. Reynolds and B. R. Noon. "Patterns of Temporal Variation in Goshawk Reproduction and Prey Resources." *Journal of Raptor Research* 39 (3) (2005): 237–246.

Schnell, J. H. "Nesting Behavior and Food Habits of Goshawks in the Sierra Nevada of California. *The Condor* 60 (1958): 377–403.

Shuster W.C. "Northern Goshawk Nest Site Requirements in the Colorado Rockies." *Western Birds* 11 (1980): 89-96.

Sibley, D. A. *The Sibley Guide to Birds.* New York: Alfred A. Knopf, 2000.

Smithers, B. L., C. W. Boals, D. E. Andersen. "Northern Goshawk Diet in Minnesota: An Analysis Using Video Recording Systems." *Journal of Raptor Research* 39 (3) (2005): 264–273.

Speiser, R., and T. Bosakowski. "Nest Site Selection by Northern Goshawks in Northern New Jersey and Southeastern New York." *The Condor* 89 (1987): 387–394.

Squires, J. "Carrion Use by Northern Goshawk." *Journal of Raptor Research* 29 (4) (1995): 283.

Squircs, J. R. and P. Kennedy. "Northern Goshawk Ecology: An Assessment of Current Knowledge and Information Needs for Conservation and Management." *Studies in Avian Biology* 31 (1986): 8–62.

Squires, J. R. and R. T. Reynolds. "Northern Goshawk," *The Birds of North America* 298, (1997).

Store: R. R. W. "Weight, Wing Area, and Skeletal Proportions in Three Accipiters." Acta XI Congress of International Ornithology (1955): 287–290.

Storer, R. W. "Sexual Dimorphism and Food Habits in Three North American Accipiters." *Auk* 83 (1966): 423–36.

Storer, R. W. "Variation in the Resident Sharp-shinned Hawks of Mexico." *The Condor* 54 (1952): 283–28.

Sutton, G. M. "Notes on the Nesting of Goshawk in Potter County, Pennsylvania." *Wilson Bull* 37 (1925): 193–199.

Sutton, G. M. "The Status of Goshawk in Pennsylvania." *Wilson Bull* 43 (1931): 108–113.

Terres, J. K. *The Audubon Society Encyclopedia of North American Birds.* New York: Alfred A. Knof, 1982.

Thrailkill, J. A., L. S. Andrews, and R. M. Claremont. "Diet of Breeding Northern Goshawks in the Coastal Range of Oregon." *Journal of Raptor Research* 34 (2000) (4): 339–340.

Underwood, J., C. M. White, and R. L. Rodriguez. "Winter Movement and Habitat Use of Northern Goshawks Breeding in Utah." *Studies in Avian Biology* 31 (2006): 228–238.

US Department of Interior, Fish and Wildlife Service. "Endangered and threatened wildlife and plants: 90-day finding for petition to list the northern goshawk in the contiguous United States west of the 100th meridian." Federal Register. 62 (188) (1997): 50892–50896.

Weins, J. D., B. R. Noon., and R. T. Reynolds. "Post-Fledging Survival of Northern Goshawks: The Importance of Prey Abundance, Weather, and Dispersal." *Ecology Applications* 16 (1) (2006): 406–418.

Wells, D. E. *100 Birds and How They Got Their Name.* Chapel Hill, NC: Algonquin Books of Chapel Hill, 2002.

Wheeler, B. K., and W. S. Clark. *A Photographic Guide to North American Raptors.* San Diego: Academic Press, 1995.

Wood, M. "Food and Measurments of Goshawks." *Auk* 55 (1938): 123–124.

Zachel, C. R. "Food Habits, Hunting Activity, and Post Fledgling Behavior of Northern Goshawks (*Accipiter gentiles*) in Interior Alaska." M.S. thesis (1985), University of Alaska, Fairbanks.